PORTFOLIO

ROKDA

Nikhil Inamdar is a Mumbai-based financial journalist. He was a prime time news presenter with NDTV Profit and worked for several years as a television correspondent at other reputed news channels after completing a postgraduate degree in broadcast journalism from the UK. He is currently consultant columnist at Business Standard Online. This is his first book.

Nikhil can be reached on email at nikhil385@gmail.com and his Twitter handle: @nik_inamdar.

HOW BANIYAS DO BUSINESS

ROKDA

NIKHIL INAMDAR

PORTFOLIO
PENGUIN

An imprint of Penguin Random House

PORTFOLIO

USA | Canada | UK | Ireland | Australia
New Zealand | India | South Africa | China | Singapore

Portfolio is part of the Penguin Random House group of companies whose addresses can be found at global.penguinrandomhouse.com

Published by Penguin Random House India Pvt. Ltd
4th Floor, Capital Tower 1, MG Road,
Gurugram 122 002, Haryana, India

Penguin Random House India

Published by Random House India in 2014

20 19 18 17 16 15 14

The views and opinions expressed in this book are the author's own and the facts are as reported by him which have been verified to the extent possible, and the publishers are not in any way liable for the same.

ISBN 9788184005899

Typeset in Electra LT by R. Ajith Kumar
Printed at Repro India Limited

www.penguin.co.in

FSC www.fsc.org MIX Paper from responsible sources FSC® C047271

This is a legitimate digitally printed version of the book and therefore might not have certain extra finishing on the cover.

For my big, fat, thriving, shining Indian household

CONTENTS

INTRODUCTION

The 'Baniya' is a loosely used expression in India, employed interchangeably to refer to the corner shop kiranawallah, the calculating money lender or the quintessential Marwari businessman next door. The connotation is often negative, but the etymology of the word is found in the Sanskrit term, vānij, which simply means trader or merchant. Originating primarily in the northern and western parts of India, the Baniyas have historically been engaged in professions ranging from money lending, commodities trading, stock broking, and shop keeping. In the present day however, they straddle sectors of the modern economy as varied as internet enabled retail, mobile telephony, and oil and gas exploration.

They are a separate Indian caste with specific sub-castes—Maheshwaris, Agarwalas etc, religious affiliations—Hindu and Jain, distinctive social customs, also have typical surnames on the basis of the clan to which they belong—Bansal, Mittal, Singhal, Goel, Garg and so on. In a wider context, the term Baniya is also used in parts of the country to refer to a conglomeration of people from diverse geographical and religious backgrounds, engaged broadly in commerce.

When I was approached to do this book that would feature the growth stories of five Baniya entrepreneurs, the first thought that crossed my mind was whether entrepreneurship could be dissected from the prism of caste alone. Could I possibly use old social segregations and hierarchies as a basis to pick a group of entrepreneurs and tell their stories? Wouldn't that only restate community stereotypes that may or may not hold true any longer?

As I began approaching people I was interested in featuring in the book, one young whiz kid—whose online restaurant-discovery portal had just received millions of dollars in private equity funding—banged the phone down on me asking never to call again. 'Baniyas in business?! Why would you want to categorize me in that manner?' he almost shrieked, evidently annoyed at my appeal to let his new-age success story be identified by the caste to which he was born.

If for a moment that incident made me circumspect about this project, all my doubts subsided once I began the interviews. For every person that was dismissive of the role their community may have played in influencing the choices they made in life, I met five others who reiterated the conscious and imperceptible weight that caste-based idiosyncrasies had on their psyche. That is not to say that those featured in this book are solely or even primarily defined by their Baniya identity. Far from it actually! After all modernity and the global nature of enterprise will have blunted old typecasts and altered our DNA considerably, wouldn't it?

But to fully discount the peculiarities of a clan established by generations of cultural and organizational frameworks would be arrogant and ill-conceived. Which is why, uncovering through these case studies why the Baniyas in particular could have long held hegemony on Indian enterprise, and continue to remain such a dominating force in the orb of commerce and trade was an exciting endeavor. From their stomach for risk and high trust culture to the strong joint family and community support infrastructure that could enable their initial rise, from their amazing ability to adapt and adjust well in unfamiliar environments to their penchant for keeping a close tab on costs and spend conscientiously; there are more positive stereotypes about the Baniyas that hold true than don't.

'They have an intrinsic understanding of money and commerce. Business is second nature to them' reckons Kunal Bahl of Snapdeal.com. He is surrounded by Baniyas—from his own partner Rohit, to all his competitors that inhabit India's e-commerce landscape. But, it is what Rohit Bansal himself shared with me that strikes a deeper chord. The community he says is inherently comfortable with uncertainty, and remains undaunted by the constant oscillations in their financial circumstances. What a virtue that is for a good businessman to have!

The five stories in this book—of the men behind Emami, Snapdeal, Meru Cabs, Hindware, and Bansal Classes—seek to bring out the matchless ingenuity of this community, and demonstrate through them how the Baniya has evolved with times, whilst continuing to retain his own unique cultural identity. I attempt to do this without necessarily keeping the caste factor at the fore, but with hope that the spirit of the Baniya DNA, which is wired for enterprise, will shine through in the narrative time and again.

The companies I've chosen not only represent different sectors of the Indian economy, but also the changing landscape of doing business in India. Emami and Hindware are brands that have withstood the test of time, blossomed in the face of cataclysmic changes. Meru Cabs and Snapdeal symbolize the spectacular opportunity liberalization has afforded to entrepreneurship and Bansal Classes is a tale of triumph in adversity.

July 16, 2014

THE MILLIONAIRE CABBIE

NEERAJ GUPTA – MERU CABS

Circa 2006—It was a regular day at work. Neeraj Gupta was in a meeting at his sprawling, newly acquired office in Goregaon when the dreaded call first came.

'Come out and take a look...' hollered that familiar intimidating voice on the other side of the line. Gupta skipped a heartbeat and rushed out, dashing down the stairs to the garage below, praying to the lord to give him strength to face what was about to greet him.

The scene he witnessed still flashes like a strobe in his memory. Broken windows, cracked windshields, and splintered glass on the floor—the brand new garage below the office, where he parked his fleet of taxis, had been rummaged through by one of the biggest names in Mumbai underworld. Gun shots had been fired, property had been damaged, a business for which Gupta had given his sweat and blood was being seized up literally. His life was in grave danger.

ONE DAY, 24 HOURS

The first set of calls had started a year earlier. On the morning of 26 July 2005 to be precise—the fateful day that ravaged Mumbai as torrential rains inundated the city, causing large-scale destruction of life and property. Curiously, just the night before, four of Neeraj's vehicles had met with fatal accidents all at once, forcing him to spend the entire night at Lilavati Hospital in Bandra, attending to his staff.

'One of the drivers has died,' a shaken Neeraj remembers telling wife Farhat on the phone, perplexed at how four vehicles from his staff transportation business were involved in mishaps on one single night. She asked him to come home early, sounding anxious. He did, but only the next morning—weary and fatigued. And just as he was about to crash into bed the cell phone rang.

'*Dubai se baat kar raha hoon...*,' someone said in Hindi. It wasn't a voice Gupta recognized, but the tone was telling enough. Thankfully, the minute he uttered 'Dubai', Gupta had the presence of mind to start recording the conversation.

'*Do crore*,' the man threatened and hung up, elaborating no further. His instinct had been proven correct. It was an extortion call asking him to pay up.

Everything that could go wrong did on that day. Mumbai was devastated by such a ferocious downpour that by 4 pm large parts of the city had completely flooded, Neeraj lost contact with his wife and would have to walk chest deep in water for hours, looking for his missing family. It didn't stop at that. A dozen more of his cars were smashed beyond repair as the garage was inundated by water.

'Even the newspapers had splashed photos of one of our car wrecks on the front page,' Gupta remembers. 'The accident, the underworld threats, the terror of a missing family, and large scale financial losses—I was staring at, it was easily the worst day of my life, and I still shudder when I think of it.'

Ironically it is this day of adversity that also proved to be a turning point for Gupta in life, and particularly in business.

GROWING UP

Neeraj Gupta was born in Mumbai in a family of second generation entrepreneurs. His grandfather's story is a quintessential rags to riches saga.

'As many unemployed young men in those days would, he boarded a train from Lucknow to arrive in (then) Bombay, with pretty much nothing but a suitcase in hand and a family to feed,' Gupta's father would tell him. In the course of the next few years he established a flourishing business, owning by the time of his passing, a chain of 14 eateries across the city—little shops in cinema halls, outside railway stations, and crowded business districts that sold snacks and tea to office goers. It was hard work, but it propelled the family out of poverty.

Neeraj's father, Vishnu Kumar Puranchan Gupta himself, a docile, happy-go-lucky man, wasn't really a desirous contender who harboured any ambition to steer the business into the big league. But the family always led a comfortable, middle-class life. With his grandfather's untimely death at the age of 40, it was Neeraj's uncle who handled the trade, running all but one restaurant, and eventually changing his line of business entirely to get into the manufacturing of corrugated boxes.

The one restaurant his father did inherit was leased out to a 'Shetty' man to run. Vishnu was a carefree soul and had decided very early on in life that making money and doing business did not excite him. Endowed sufficiently with an inheritance and with a steady income from the restaurant he had leased out, he spent his days pursuing other interests—which meant starting his day with a morning swim at the Mafatlal Club on Charni Road, an afternoon session of badminton at Khar Gymkhana, evenings at the Santacruz club, playing billiards, and finally calling it a day with a game of cards with his friends. Quite evidently, the family wasn't swiftly climbing the ladder of monetary success, but, were a happy and contented lot.

If business had skipped Vishnu's genes, there was enough of it happening around Neeraj for the seed of enterprise to be sown somewhere. Whether within the paternal side of the family, or in his mother's maternal home where the *nana* and *mamas* operated steel mills and ready garment stores, people were always engaged in some entrepreneurial activity or the other. Neeraj never knew anyone who did a job. And so right from the early days, it was very clear to him that he will not work for someone else, but create something of his own.

A creator he was of trouble, mischief, and commotion for starters! At the age of five, he walked two kilometers from school to a hospital, unaccompanied, to see his new born sister. By seven he had almost burnt the house down while playing with fire. His adventurous streak made him a hugely popular kid, famous for organizing festivals, *dandiya nights*, and New Year parties in the modest MHADA building where the Guptas lived. He enjoyed being at the forefront, bossing around friends, delegating work, and managing events. So popular did their events become in the next few years, that they even started garnering sponsorships, drawing crowds of more than three thousand people. These activities continued right through college and the young boy even managed to make good money occasionally.

'I remember raking in Rs 20,000 for a college fest that we organized. In 1991, for a teenager still to hit twenty, that was a princely sum,' reminisces a grinning Neeraj.

College was a breeze—a 'paid holiday' Gupta calls it—spent hanging around campus and the canteen. 'A girlfriend by our side on day one!' proclaimed a friend of his, as they geared up for the first day of college at Mithibai. The dogged determination, aside of finishing a B. Com degree, was to get a girlfriend. And so, filmy as it may sound, Gupta fell in love on day one, and started wooing Farhat—now his wife—on day two.

With no pressure from home to excel in academics or follow a particular stream of discipline, he was an average student at best, more interested in girlfriends, extracurricular activities and in pursuing a myriad different hobbies, which on most occasions he managed to successfully monetize.

The first of these sideline fads that caught his fancy was inspired by a gentleman he met on a family holiday. 'He sold us a grain of rice with an inscription on it and I instantly thought—why can't I do this as well? And so I did it—gifting one to my thoroughly impressed girlfriend,' Gupta laughs. He was also crafting these by the dozen for friends who implored him with requests to flatter the ladies, and even sold in bulk to a trader who peddled them at stores like Archies and Hallmark that were all the rage back in the day.

'I will pay you Rs 20 a piece. Make me 500 of these,' the trader told him. And so, Neeraj got his first paycheck crafting 500 assiduously inscribed one-liners on rice grain. It made him richer by Rs 10,000. The moneymaking seed was in him right from childhood. 'I am sick of having to travel in the trains. I will be jet-setting around the world first-class one day, mark my words,' he would tell his mother, in school.

'*Ja re...kitni badi baatein karta hai*,' she would scold in Hindi.

By the third year of college, Farhat had a job with Jet Airways as cabin crew. Her father passed away early and she took it up to support her family. Neeraj too graduated with a decent score and with ample time on hand with not much to do. He wasn't travelling first-class yet, but his routine now revolved around flight arrivals and departures. He was Farhat's official chauffeur, dropping her off to and picking her up from the airport, much to the chagrin of his otherwise composed parents.

'You must do something, Neeraj. This is not the age to be sitting at home,' his father said at last. 'A friend of mine runs a textile manufacturing company, I have spoken to him about you, and he has agreed to have you on board.'

And so with no good enough reason to defy his dad, Gupta reluctantly began work at Tunicas. It was the first and the only time he worked for somebody else. Three months was how long the stint lasted.

IN BUSINESS

Around Diwali that year, Neeraj's new company was handing out little gifts to employees—those classic faux-leather boxes with a pen, a key chain and a wallet. That souvenir, he says, proved to be a trigger for his first serious, grown-up business venture and a chance to get out of a boring job.

A friend of Neeraj's sister, working at the time for Hindustan Unilever had come home one evening. Neeraj was lounging around, passing time after work, when he overheard the friend telling his sister about a product launch for which her boss had asked her to think of ideas for corporate gifting.

'I can't think of anything appropriate for the occasion,' she said. 'Any ideas Neeraj?'

He rushed in at once, opened his bag and handed over the

present he'd had received at office. 'I can supply as many of these as you want,' he said, not thinking for a moment where from and how he was going to source the leather boxes.

'Ok. I will take this along and show it to my manager.'

Surely the next day he got a call from the HUL head office asking him to come over for a meeting.

'How much would these cost?' asked the manager. Neeraj stared at him blank as a wall, with not a clue as to how much he should quote.

'Rs 800,' he said, taking a leap of faith.

'Will you be able to supply in bulk?' asked the manager.

'Yes!' said Neeraj, surprised at his own confidence about accomplishing a job about which he knew nothing.

'Okay, let's do this,' the manager said within a fraction of a second. 'I will issue a P.O. (purchase order) for 500 pieces. What company do you represent?'

'Delta Exports,' Neeraj blurted out, as if on cue. He is still not quite sure just how that name popped up in his head out of the blue, but sure as hell, at age 21, he had bagged his first big order of Rs 4 lakh, for a product he knew nothing about and in the name of a company that was but a figment of his wacky imagination. He was thrilled!

The product was a hit and Delta Exports got repeat orders from HUL. Within a span of three months, the company had made a killing—a profit of Rs 3 lakh, a figure that was several times more than his salary at Tunicas.

The business was a huge learning experience for Gupta. Not only had he proved to himself that he had the capability to confidently deal with large customers, but also that he could do business with integrity, and still make a comfortable margin, having been determined to execute an all-white transaction in a trade where black money was the norm.

With a swagger in his stride and a sizable amount of money in the bank, he handed in his resignation, setting out to spend the next three years toying with no less than seven-eight different business ideas—from exporting embroidered garments to setting up a new company (ingeniously named Willow Paper Craft) manufacturing paper bags.

Some worked, others didn't, but the money he made selling leather gift cases to HUL sustained these experiments till he turned twenty four, giving him a chance to dabble in a number of small ventures. His only mantra was, no matter which business he got into, he would recover his investment, make a reasonable margin, and never lose money—a fundamental rule he adheres to, till date.

THE GARAGE GUY

In 1998, Neeraj and Farhat got married. His was the first inter-religious marriage in a family where nobody had yet had a love marriage. To his surprise, despite their conservative background, his parents did not oppose the match.

Farhat's traditional Muslim family though, was aghast. 'So much so, that her brothers and uncles threatened to kill me if we went ahead with the ceremony. But no threats were going to stop us from getting married and so in full filmy style, with the drama quotient high as always, the wedding happened under full police protection,' Gupta recalls with much amusement.

Having exhausted all his cash though on a big-bang wedding, and after trying his hand at multiple businesses, professionally things were back to square one. With Farhat having changed jobs, moving from Jet Airways to British Airways the only thing that changed was that instead of chauffeuring his girlfriend from college to domestic airport, he was now ferrying his wife around from home to the international airport.

Joblessness though was soon beginning to affect him and even became an embarrassment for Farhat who was not quite sure what to say when people asked her what her husband was up to.

'You need to make a definite start somewhere, Neeraj,' she said one day.

'I've been thinking about an idea. My friend Arun Shetty who services our cars has approached me for a partnership to open a service garage,' Gupta told her.

'A garage!?' she exclaimed.

'Yes, there is a lot that can be done in this space to formalize the existing set up.'

'How much is the investment?'

'He is putting in Rs, 50,000, and I will have to put in the same amount. We are doing a 50:50 partnership.'

Farhat dished into her savings and gave Neeraj the money without batting an eyelid. And that is how Elite Class Garage was founded in late 1998.

The garage industry at that point was a large, informal trade with very little agreeable about it from a customer standpoint. Neeraj would often harangue Arun, who worked for one of the garages in the city and serviced his father's car, about how the existing model could be changed for the better and how corporate clients who wanted a value add in the service delivered to them was a segment that was largely untapped. Their conversations had got Arun thinking, and that is how he approached Neeraj to partner him.

With a lakh rupees in capital raised between the two of them, the duo got into business straight away. They bought tools and paid half the amount as deposit for a shed in Oshiwara—a neighborhood full of unauthorized automobile repair shops. The idea was to remain in the thick of all the action, differentiate in the middle of competition, rather than do business in an isolated part of town. In a trade where there was no discernible feature that one could consider to tell apart the hundreds of *repairwallahs* in the vicinity, Neeraj and Arun got thinking on how they could do things another way.

The first thing they did to stand apart, was to set up a small cabin in the garage where they could entertain clients. Where customers next door were sweating it out and getting uncomfortable in a greasy, grimy shack, refusing to sit on the dirty plastic chairs strewn about for the fear of having their clothes soiled, Neeraj and Arun were enlightening clients about their 'premium services' over a cup of tea and biscuits.

They came out with annual membership offers, loyalty

cards, and scores of freebies bundled in with their service packages which included small things like six free car washes per annum, toeing services, oil change at no cost etc. They were small but significant value adds that helped them make a distinction and capture customers without charging too much more than their competitors. They also realized that for reliable service, the customer was willing to pay a small premium.

Within a matter of months there was lot of work coming in. Over 200 clients had signed up on annual memberships and business was on a roll. Neeraj, however, wasn't a mechanic by profession and beyond a point would get bored sitting in office twiddling his thumbs. Oshiwara, was in those days largely an industrial zone, but with many corporate offices, BPOs (Business Process Outsourcing) and multinational companies setting up base in the area. Blue Dart, Tata Infotech, and Sony were among companies that had their headquarters right across the road from Neeraj and Arun's garage. He immediately spotted an opportunity here. The logical next step to grow was to acquire retainer corporate clients who serviced their fleet only at authorized dealerships, by offering them the same service at a much cheaper rate.

Gupta soon began seeking appointments with these companies. Turning up at their offices impeccably dressed, he would prod them with bulk discounts, so that they would shift business from authorized dealerships. He convinced them not to dispose off their old vehicles, which he promised he would restore to as good as new. Clients were impressed with the idea of a well turned-out garage owner, speaking with them in clear English and also the value-for-money proposals they were being lured them with. He positioned his service as an in-between. If an authorized dealer charged Rs 1000 for a repair and a local garage charged Rs 500 for the same service, Elite Class would charge Rs 650-700 combining low operational costs with a professional approach and faultless service.

'We soon had clients signing up by the dozens, with a battery of 20 cars lined up outside their office at any given point, waiting to be serviced much to the chagrin of other rivals,' Gupta says.

But a garage was after all a garage, and Neeraj Gupta, the itchy, restless being that he was, wasn't about to spend his lifetime in a car repair workshop!

The creative and monetary limitations of the business started niggling him soon enough, bringing him at crossroads yet again—scaling up meant acquiring more land and resources, which in turn meant more capital investments. The financial aspect could still be taken care of, but the thought of being a *garagewallah* all his life was bothering him somewhere at the back of his mind. What he really wanted to do at this point was associate firmly in some way or the other with a strong corporate brand and become an exclusive travel vendor rather than a mere service provider.

This wasn't difficult. Gupta's personal relationships with Elite Class's corporate clients were only going from strength to strength because of his affable, easy-going nature. And it was as a result of one of these associations that he formed Travel Link, now known as V-Link Travel Solutions, the holding company of Meru Cabs, the brand that he is famous for today.

Back then, in its initial avatar, it was basically a company that owned one shuttle coach and employed two people—a cleaner and a driver to ferry BPO workers across the city.

RIDING THE BPO WAVE

The year 2000 was when the BPO boom had just taken off in India, with several American as well as Indian multinational companies setting up back offices and call centers in Indian cities, making it a global hub for outsourcing. This explosion of back offices not only created huge employment opportunities for young professionals and a demand for swanky office spaces, but also for shuttle services and cabs to ferry the large pool of employees working odd hours.

Tata Infotech (which was later merged with TCS or Tata Consultancy Services) was coming out with a tender for one such executive shuttle coach to provide transfers for its employees in five of its offices in the city. The administration head of the company immediately got in touch with Neeraj and asked him to put in a bid. He won the tender for a five-year contract which entailed operating a state-of-art fourteen-seater air conditioned coach.

Neeraj had a customized bus ready in no time, equipped with TV screens, writing boards, microphones, reading lights and a refrigerator—it was 'beautiful and one of its kind in those days. Even the Managing Director came to inaugurate it' he remembers with pride.

But undertaking this contract meant saying goodbye to the garage, as his partner Arun, was unwilling to shell out the Rs 14 lakh investment needed to buy the bus. Between Farhat and himself, Neeraj managed to raise Rs 3 lakh needed for the 25 percent down payment and took a loan for the rest of the amount. While it was a big risk at that point in time, in hindsight it was the best decision he had made.

The thumb rule in the car rental business is that the cost of a vehicle should be recovered from roughly a year's revenues. With a single bus in its fleet, Travel Link, was to be sure bringing in revenues of Rs 1 lakh a month and a tidy profit of Rs 50,000 for Neeraj, after paying off EMIs and salaries. With Farhat also bringing home a handsome pay packet, the two were, in today's lingo, the quintessential turn of century DINK (double income, no kids) couple, having a time of their life. But this was just a teaser. Success in its true sense, that would take the business to soaring heights and catapult Gupta into a different league altogether, was yet to come.

Travel Link's growth trajectory pretty much coincided with the hectic pace of growth in the BPO industry and it was only a matter of time before the lakhs on its balance sheet morphed into crores. One bus soon became two, and two became four and soon enough as BPOs expanded their back offices across cities like Delhi, Chennai, and Bangalore, Neeraj too was spreading his tentacles to capture these new markets as a travel services provider.

As the outsourcing industry expanded and late-night call centers flourished, thousands of workers scattered across the length and breadth of the country, working late-night shifts had to be picked up from fifty different points in each city, which meant companies had to deploy scores of cabs. The Tata Infotech connection, where he had started out with a contract of barely 10-15 vehicles taken on dry lease in Mumbai, helped. The reputation he had built there for honesty, clean dealings, and faultless service-delivery ensured that Neeraj had almost all the BPOs signing up with him. He soon had to expand rapidly to cater to scores of other back offices of companies like JP Morgan, EDS, Daksh etc.

Soon, even as competition started heating up and several other players, wanting to cash-in on the opportunity, tried to make aggressive inroads, undercutting and using all sorts of tactics to compete for contracts, Gupta managed to stay ahead of the curve.

How?

He used the very same principle that he had during the garage days—constant value-add. He introduced what were then considered unique concepts like safety training, driver identity cards, uniforms, car supervisors on site to ensure smooth operations, annual dinners for clients at five star hotels as relationship building exercises, and unmatched service delivery. With Farhat on flights three to four days a week, Gupta plunged himself entirely into work, dedicating 12-14 hours in personally supervising operations.

The motto was to deliver on commitments by hook or by

crook. So, sometimes when he was short of a car he'd borrow his parents or in-laws' vehicle. Very often, if there were guests from abroad in need of an English speaking driver, he'd chauffeur them around in his own Maruti Esteem. 'I had no qualms doing this. You have to be completely involved in your business and if need be, get your hands dirty as well. The day you start running it superficially it will suffer,' Gupta says.

The business model was straightforward—Gupta's company would liaise with car suppliers, and play the role of an aggregator to ensure that service quality was maintained. The idea was to keep the business asset light and so only a few of the vehicles were to be owned by the company. He had as many as 1300 vehicles on the road, but by 2006, with business on a roll and vehicle ownership becoming a critical selling-point for vendors, Travel Link had to purchase and maintain hundred vehicles of its own. This would, as Gupta realized later, prove to be a burden rather than a blessing, as problems of parking, maintenance, drivers on the pay rolls, frequent accidents etc. would keep him awake all night.

In the larger scheme of things though, these were just teething issues in what was otherwise a blooming business. A large part of the success was a function of being at the right place at the right time. Travel Link was only riding the dot com wave, growing in tandem with the BPO industry. What helped it sustain the momentum and gather scale though was the dedication and risk taking capacity of the man who ran it. Neeraj never dithered from ploughing back the money he was making into his business.

In a span of just a few years, the company was growing in rapid multiples of five-six times. Between 2000 and 2001, annual turnover grew ten times from Rs 12 lakh to roughly Rs 1.2 cr and by 2005-2006, Travel Link had a top line of Rs 43 Cr, with operations in five cities. Initially, operating with just one driver and one cleaner from home, Neeraj now employed 200-odd people across the country and worked out of his sprawling 4000-square feet office in Goregaon.

'In a shot I also shifted into a swanky six bedroom apartment in Andheri, spending a whopping Rs 1 cr just on interiors,' he smiles.

But with success came its ugly baggage of problems that almost threatened to scuttle the existence of Gupta's booming enterprise.

The shooting incident happened in 2006.

While it was nearly a year after the first call from Dubai, it proved to be the proverbial last nail in the coffin. The underworld threats had persisted despite the fact that the family had full police protection, including two cops at Gupta's side at all times. His case was also being looked into by the Anti-Extortion cell, but the police got fed up of the calls and told him there was nothing much they could do to stop the menace, as he had already been given two bodyguards, a licensed rifle and were doing all they could to keep him safe.

With two little daughters and a wife at home, work piling up in office and constant stress about the safety of his family, life had become a living hell. Farhat even suggested that the family move to London, where the couple had friends, who could help them settle initially. She was at that time, working as cabin crew for British Airways and frequently travelled to the United Kingdom. Neeraj was disturbed at the thought of shifting bag and baggage to London, even though somewhere in the back of his mind the thought of a safe environment for the girls was a comforting idea.

As luck would have it, London never happened, and within a few months of the shootout the threats faded out. Neeraj was convinced he wouldn't pay a single penny of ransom and he stuck to that resolve. They eventually gave up. But the pressure was intense and it took a toll on him mentally. The intimidation had stopped, but his passion and zeal to grow his business also ebbed out swiftly. Those 24 hours between the 25 and 26 of July 2005—and the terrible year after that, till the shooting incident at office was the worst period of his life. But through this adversity, also came the big opportunity he was looking for all along.

'I was provoked to disrupt the status quo. In due course, I got so fed up that I firmed up my decision to scout for an investor and sell out.' That investor, which Gupta was seeking to cash out of Travel Link, would end up becoming a key force behind the Meru story.

But little did he know that back then.

THE GOVERNMENT TENDER

Around the time he was getting ready to fold, Travel Link, Neeraj hired Mind Spring, an investment advisory firm, to scout for a buyer. Through them he met Vikram Nirula. Vikram and Vishal Nevatia, former Arthur Anderson employees, had quit their jobs in 1999 to co-found GW Capital, the antecedent of IVFA or India Value Fund Advisors. IVFA, with investments in a dozen marquee names apart from Meru, was a firm that liked to do controlled transactions, whereby it could hold a majority stake, take the business to a certain scale, professionalize it and then exit in a five-seven year timeframe.

With Meru they approached things a little differently.

'We used a more venture capital rather than PE approach,'" says Nirula, who with hindsight believes that the investment could have happened in 2010 rather than 2007, but cautions that sometimes you need to be ignorant about the market realities and throw caution to the winds if you are to make a success out of a very difficult, but exciting business. 'If you know too much about a business, you will think only about the difficulties,' he adds.

Gupta's first meeting with Vikram was a debacle. He rejected Travel Link's buyout proposal right away saying IVFA was not interested in the B2B staff transportation space owing to concerns about scaling up. Several other players in the private equity world had also responded to him in a similar manner.

Neeraj's option to pack his bags and leave was suddenly no longer available. He thought he had hit rock bottom with all doors closing on him. But quietly, a bigger one had opened. That fateful meeting with Vikram, even though he didn't know it yet, would change his life quite dramatically. Around this time—in May 2006 to be precise, another opportunity had landed at his doorstep and that is where the two would end up collaborating.

Neeraj was in office going about his usual morning routine one day when a colleague excitedly barged into his cabin. 'Look at this,' he said, pointing to a newspaper advertisement. 'The state government is coming out with a tender to give out licenses for new AC fleet taxis. Should we apply?'

'Put in a bid,' said Neeraj disinterestedly, not enquiring about the nitty-gritty of the tender process, when it was decided that the company would throw in a proposal. He was still wallowing in dejection, with very little of his brain focused on what was happening in business.

This was the time of the Vilas Rao Deshmukh administration, which was working on hectic plans for the city's makeover. The Chief Minister's officials were deeply absorbed in working on a much-touted dream of turning Mumbai into Shanghai—a plan that was presided over by one Mr Sanjay Ubale, the then Secretary of Special Projects—Maharashtra State. As it is now widely recognized, while Mumbai is still a distant dream away from becoming Shanghai, the bid to give Mumbai's rusty old cabs a facelift as a part of this vision fructified, making along the way, a millionaire out of the small- time garage owner who wanted to pack his bags and leave for London.

Travel Link applied for the license, and much to their surprise won the bid. 'There cannot have been more than two or three applicants at the time,' says Gupta.

In 2006, there were virtually no players in the radio taxi business and the closest thing to what the Maharashtra government had in mind was someone like Travel Link with its 1,500 odd cars and solid experience in operating a fleet of air-conditioned cabs. The magnitude of this opportunity had still not hit Neeraj. It was only after an initial meeting with the concerned department in the government to understand the business model that Gupta realized what a coup it had been and what a goldmine he was sitting on.

For anyone familiar with Mumbai, the battered old black and yellow cabs—rickety Premier Padminis from the early 60s, knackered Maruti vans and now an assortment of small hatchbacks like the Santro—are an iconic, distinctive insignia of the city. 50,000 of them still crisscross its roads, carrying passengers from one point to another. While they give a unique nostalgic flavor to the visiting tourist, adding to the character of Mumbai, practically speaking, they are well past their 'use-by' date. They are muggy, smelly, the meters are faulty, there is no air-conditioning, and quite a few of them are also unsafe to run much longer. For a city that has for long harbored dreams of turning itself into Shanghai, they continue to remain an anachronism on the roads.

After the initial indifference, Gupta was suddenly keyed up. The government had opened up a fiercely-guarded sector and he didn't want to let go of the opportunity. Having travelled abroad frequently with his wife, he would always be in awe of the modern, state-of-the-art transportation systems in use there. Clean, air-conditioned cabs with GPS and GPRS technologies, tamper-proof meters that printed e-bills and strictly prescribed fare structures, with no scope for being taken for a ride by drivers. The thought of starting a cab service on these lines had crossed his mind several times, but government restrictions had always come in the way. Now, the opportunity had literally come walking to his doorstep.

'And the license was for 10,000 cabs. That was the figure that really tickled me. I realized that this had the potential to be a game changer and a chance to transform the extant landscape which was dominated by the old, rusty black and yellow cabs. Suddenly after months of being in a state of gloom, I was bubbling with excitemen!'

Equipped with a license in tow, Neeraj and his team, once again made their way to the India Value Fund office—this time, not with a plea to sell the staff transportation business, but to seek fresh funding for the radio taxi venture.

Travel Link had excellent relationships with its banks and an impressive balance sheet to boast of, so getting an initial loan sanctioned for a new company was not a problem. Seed capital was not a hurdle, as banks were more than willing to extend recourse financing. But 10,000 cabs, even though it was a long haul, entailed massive investment and there was no way he could have raised the requisite capital on his own. A simple, back of the envelope calculation of Rs 5 lakh per car multiplied by 10,000 meant the business would need around Rs 500 cr, of which Rs 50-60 Cr would be required straight away. The best bet was to induct a PE partner.

Vikram and Vishal shared Gupta's vision and were quickly convinced about the fact that this license could potentially revolutionize a sector that was virtually free of competition. A big convincing point for Travel Link was also the fact that they already had operations of 500 to 600 vehicles in Mumbai for the staff transportation business. So, even if this venture was to fail, with passengers unwilling to pay a higher premium for radio taxis, the cars could be used during the night for the call centers, ensuring that losses, if any, could be minimized and no vehicle remained underutilized. Even in a worst case scenario of zero demand from retail consumers, business from Travel Link could still be used to cover costs and help pay off the EMIs.

This fall-back arrangement, which was in effect a combination of both B2B and B2C models, gave much confidence to the IVF team. It was also a win-win scenario for Gupta's corporate clients who would benefit from a new fleet of vehicles equipped with the latest technology.

Finally, after detailed negotiations over two months, India Value Fund came on board in August 2006, with an initial investment of Rs 10 Cr in the form of convertible debentures. It was essentially a type of debt to be converted into equity after a year if certain business targets were met, or repaid in full or if things didn't go according to plan. It was a big risk, because in event of failure, Neeraj would have had to literally forgo his entire profit for the next two years to pay off IVF's dues.

But he was willing to take the chance.

A MERU ON THE ROAD

On 30 March 2007, ten months after Neeraj had reluctantly put in a bid, the Meru was finally launched with a media blitzkrieg. The who's who of the city were present at the event with the then Chief Minister of Maharashtra, Vilas Rao Deshmukh, presiding over the function as the chief guest and veteran actor and danseuse Hema Malini performing for the occasion. The star-studded turnout ensured extensive media coverage with newspapers going gaga over Mumbai's first ritzy, air-conditioned cab. The promise of mild mannered drivers displaying their ID cards on the dashboards and strict decrees like 'I will not drink and drive' 'I will be well-groomed', and 'I will charge the customer as per the meter' were a first of its kind, and the press lapped up the offering.

The next morning, on day one, Meru's call centre was flooded with enquiries and the phone didn't stop ringing for the entire day. The company kicked off operations with barely 30 vehicles, but so enormous was the demand that the call centre was averaging about 500 calls per day. In the first week alone, booking requests were four or five times the capacity the company could make available. Neeraj and company realized very early on that the only way to survive and stay relevant was to expand rapidly and reduce order rejection volumes. Speed was the key.

'The killer in this business is to refuse a customer. That leaves a very bad taste and you may lose that client for a very long time,' Gupta explains. Not wanting to be faced with such a scenario, V-Link, in a shot placed an order for a thousand Maruti Esteem cars. They had initially bought a fleet of merely fifty in order to test the market, but by the end of March 2008, with Mumbai more or less addicted to the plush, convenient Meru, even a fleet of thousand wouldn't suffice. So phenomenal was the growth, that within two years the company had two thousand of its cabs snaking around the roads of Mumbai.

But as new frontiers were being seized, old ways had to be discarded.

During the pre-launch period Neeraj had to get down to revamping the company's entire organizational structure, and forget old ways of doing business completely. With the induction of an international private equity partner, there came about radical changes which he on his own could not have imagined effecting.

'IVF brought in their own ethos and values, their world-class corporate culture, which I had never been exposed to till date. They insisted on a lot of changes that I as a sole entrepreneur would've perhaps never envisaged,' he admits with honesty.

Adjusting to this transition hurt initially though, and it took Neeraj time to accept the truth that he was no longer the sole proprietor who could take decisions at a whim. What was needed at that point for the business to flourish was high entrepreneurial energy along with induction of high quality processes that only experienced outside professionals could bring to the table.

IVF was trying to do just that and Gupta aligned to the new realities showing a maturity that not many entrepreneurs do.

One of the first things India Value Fund insisted upon was that Neeraj shift into a bigger commercial space and set up another office. A board was constituted with 3 IVF representatives and Gupta as members. Among the first decision the board collectively took was to get Accenture to write the processes, and appoint KPMG and Ernst & Young—among the world's biggest auditing companies—to keep accounts. They also hired a technology partner in Singapore for the backend and call centre and roped in an HR consultant to appoint a professional team to manage various segments of the business. At several points during this transition—from a local, individually run company to a professionally managed set up. Neeraj felt there was profligate expenditure being incurred and unnecessary processes being espoused. But he gave the other members of his board the benefit of doubt and with hindsight accepts the efficacy of some of their decisions which were critical to building a new age brand.

'He is a fundamentally savvy business person. Right at the beginning we told him of the changes we would be effecting to professionalize the set up. And he understood that for him holding a smaller stake in a larger, scaled up business would mean more value eventually than having a bigger stake in a smaller company that may perhaps have never grown,' says IVF's Nirula, who lauds Neeraj for not resisting equity dilution as a consequence of the capital intensive nature of his business.

While operational changes were effected by the board, Gupta got busy with the brand building exercise. Getting the overall positioning right and having a brand strategy in place was crucial since India did not have a precedent with Radio Taxis. V-Link signed up Chlorophyll on the job, which did a rigorous exercise with the management to understand their core philosophy and thought behind the venture. Neeraj, on the advice of a friend was only adamant about the fact that he didn't want an obvious name for the brand, but a lateral more esoteric trademark.

After several workshops and discussions it was decided that the cab would be called Meru—a mountain believed to be at the heart of the universe, the abode of Lord Brahma, and a pantheon of gods and goddesses. It was also according to ancient texts, the epicenter of the earth during the churning of the oceans (Sagar Manthan). It denoted sturdiness, reliability, and size—all vital dimensions of this business. A happy coincidence was also that Me and Ru were the first two initials of Neeraj's two daughters Mehak and Ruhi .

In order to stand out it was also decided that the cabs would be painted a bright turquoise green, which really worked in the company's favor because people did immediately take note.

Within six months of Meru's launch in Mumbai, the brand also took its next big leap. Neeraj got a call from the GMR group which was getting ready to unveil its swanky new international airport in Hyderabad. They had heard of Meru's success in Mumbai and approached him with a proposal to operate 400 taxis to and from the airport in Shamshabad. A comfortable, clean cab service was a must because the airport was 25 kilometers away from the city. Soon enough, the company was crossing one milestone after another. By the end of 2008, it launched in Delhi and had an invitation to start operations in Bengaluru. A while later it extended its services in Jaipur, Ahmedabad, and Chennai as well.

The early rise of Meru was meteoric. But alas, it wasn't too long before Gupta would have to face up to a barrage of challenges from all ends. Even as consumer demand was taking the brand from strength to strength, the operating environment was becoming increasingly tougher. A few things happened simultaneously even as the company was growing at an intense pace in the first two years.

The funding aspect, which ironically is the trickiest bit for any start up or entrepreneur was taken care of pretty quickly in the case of Gupta with IVF coming on board. So was the course of going through the bidding process where the company got extremely lucky as a result of little or no competition. The big speed bump that needed to be crossed was obtaining permits. The taxi license had come with a rider that the contractor will have to acquire permits from existing cab drivers.

It is here that Gupta's core strengths as a traditional, rooted entrepreneur—the understanding of local processes and procedures, and an ability to get things done by plotting a course through tough government bureaucracy, came to good use.

If you are to drive a metered taxi in Mumbai, you need to hold a taxi badge and a permit, which is very hard to come by. In 1997 the Bombay High Court had frozen the issuance of new permits due to pollution control and traffic management rules and also because it felt there were already too many cabs on the roads. There were roughly 1.5 lakh taxi badge holders but permits for only 60,000 black and yellow cabs, which meant the demand for them was very high.

V-Link Travel Solutions, which was the registered new holding company incorporated to start Meru's B2C taxi business, managed to obtain 200-300 of these almost immediately in order to commence operations.

'We appointed our entire company machinery to get behind permit holders. The usual practice for the owners of these permits was to lease them out for five years. But we offered to lock them in for a period of 20 years. Permit holders were only too happy to enter into a longer tenure agreement. In a bid to lure them, they were paid four times the money which was also a big added incentive,' Gupta explains.

Over the next two years, as the company expanded, they managed to get hold of as many as 2,000 permits. Nearly 1500 of those were obtained by asking the Government of Maharashtra to grant them the use of dead or lapsed permits—which are basically those that are not in use. This meant getting teams to sit across RTO offices in the city and making a list of the names and addresses of people who held these prized but dormant cards. Over months of hard work Gupta and his team built a database which revealed that there were as many as 15,000 permits not in use. Once again large teams were dispatched to each and every address in the file to try and persuade permit holders to part with their licenses. In no time, they managed to get hold of 1400-1500 permits. It was a unique and ingenious way of navigating a rather peculiar problem.

But this victory proved only to be a temporary breather.

DEFYING ALL ODDS

The politicization of the taxi permit issue in subsequent years grew to be the single biggest constraining factor for Meru in Mumbai. Meru's diversified presence helped it hedge its overall business and sail on. Things would have been much messier had they been a one city phenomenon, but that was little solace.

Growth flattened out at 2000 cars, and then saw a reversal for some years despite demand for Meru's services being very high. The sole reason for this—lack of availability of drivers holding valid permits. As if the environment wasn't bad enough, in 2010 the Maharashtra government decided to deal a further blow to radio cabs by giving new taxi permits only to those who could provide a domicile certificate proving that they had lived in Mumbai for more than 15 years and could read and write Marathi. This was done in the midst of a violent campaign launched by Maharashtra Navnirman Sena chief Raj Thackeray against North Indian migrants in the state.

'Most taxi drivers in Mumbai are from Uttar Pradesh, and

the locals do not want to drive cabs as they find better jobs. This politically motivated rule made it very difficult to find drivers not just for the fleet cabs, but even for the regular cabs,' the Bombay Taximen's association secretary A. L. Quadros complains.

Adds Neeraj, 'Across the globe, whether it is in New York, London, or Singapore, the cab drivers are almost always migrants. Such has been the case in Mumbai as well for the longest time. But the politics of regionalism superseded the politics of development, crippling Meru's prospects by 2010.'

These rules coupled with the onslaught of competition from new players like Mega Cabs, Ola Cabs, Tab Cab and others meant that the number of Meru taxis on Mumbai's roads reduced from 2000 between 2009 and 2012 to roughly 1500 by 2014. This is not because the spoils of the market had to be shared, but because poaching of drivers became common place. By creating an artificial scarcity in permits, politics had completely distorted the market and reduced the availability of drivers.

Worse still, politicians were unionizing with rogue employees who over the years held the company to ransom on more than one occasion. It started with the old guard. The black and yellow taxi drivers were not ready for struggle against this genteel breed of new taxi owners. Dissent began soon after the first lot of taxis were launched in Mumbai, starting with a one-day strike and attempts to block in courts the advent of newer cabs. That failed, so it soon turned to repeated tactics of intimidation over a period—stone pelting, breaking windshields, beating up Meru drivers etc. From time to time the tussles got so ugly that customers were even forced out of cabs by unidentified men on the road.

Over the next few years this rebellion morphed into driver unions like the Meru Cabs Chalak Sena, backed by political outfits like the Shiv Sena, or the Swabhiman Sanghatna led by the politician Nitish Rane, going on indefinite strikes to extract their pound of flesh. Across other cities like Bangalore and Hyderabad too, drivers protested against supposed coercive tactics by Meru, complaining that the company was seeking very high rentals. Cabs were set ablaze, an ex-CEO was at the receiving end of threatening calls and violent protests became a norm between 2009 and 2013.

In 2013 a prolonged strike was the sixth occasion in the company's short existence that operations had been brought to a grinding halt by a few errant drivers. It was also perhaps the most crippling one. There were 50 odd incidents of vehicles being damaged and drivers being assaulted. Meru was losing Rs 15 lakh in subscription revenue with each passing day, while drivers were collectively losing Rs 30 lakh in customer revenue.

With things getting progressively worse, Gupta decided to talk tough. Meru not only suspended the services of several drivers, but also launched aggressive press and social media campaigns through front page advertisements in major newspapers, appealing to Mumbaikars for help. 'On social media, we managed to garner overwhelming support from customers, with more than 5000 people signing up to show their solidarity. Finally after 12 days of negotiations and losses of over a crore, the strike was called off,' says Gupta, still perturbed by the memory.

Who was to blame? Was it bad policies or bad politics that was leading to such repeated disruptions? Meru's business model was simple and straightforward. It paid the driver a subscription—Rs 900-Rs1300 a day—while owning and maintaining the fleet. While it admittedly took the company time to better align the driver-organization relationship—avoiding scenarios where the driver kept all the upside, with Meru assuming the risk, or where the company profiteered unreasonably while the driver remained a mere employee, Neeraj believes that for most part it was just a case of a few bad apples who had been politically instigated to resort to violence. He says a majority of the drivers were and continue to remain supportive of the management for the earning platform they've been provided with.

Charters like the one submitted by unions in 2013 consisted of 21 explicit demands that were related to issues like subscription charges, other overheads to be paid by drivers, wrongful deduction of maintenance and repair charges, weekly offs etc. Press reports of the time and anonymous interactions with at least a dozen drivers revealed that most often decisions were unilaterally taken by top union leaders without support from majority of the drivers and any divergence in opinion from members was not tolerated. Drivers also said they are mostly happy with the company and earned anywhere between Rs 15000-Rs 20000 a month, which was at least 30 percent more than what they were making while driving the black and yellow taxis.

But Meru was losing heavily. It was spending Rs 15,000 on repair and maintenance, Rs 15,000 on fixed administration costs, and 15,000 on EMIs per vehicle, while it earned only Rs 30,000 roughly from drivers. Yielding to demands for an ever sweeter deal for drivers was not possible.

With losses swelling, the only option remaining was to tweak the business model with an intention to bring in operational efficiencies and reduce instances of agitation and strife. Attempting to side step the deep politicization of the sector became a key to survival, particularly in Mumbai where the days of heady growth were quickly nipped in the bud.

AN EVOLVING MODEL

By late 2011, despite being in business for five years, the company hadn't been able to achieve its target of putting 10,000 cabs on the road, as a result of these myriad operational problems. It was bleeding heavily, losing almost Rs 5 cr every month.

Gupta and his team realized that the crisis was as a result of a combination of factors—a hostile regulatory environment, volatile relations with drivers, and deteriorating quality of service that was leading to a consumer backlash.

It was soon decided that a new CEO must be inducted to look into the minutiae of daily operations while Neeraj, who despite continuing as the managing director, would along with the IVF team and a set of independent experts work on devising a corporate strategy to get things back on track. Siddharth Pahwa was appointed as the new man at the helm to turnaround the business. Pahwa had a strong mind of his own and had an honest chat with Neeraj right on day one about being allowed to do things his own way.

Most entrepreneurs would have resisted ceding control, preferring that the lines between ownership and management remained blurred, but Neeraj gave Siddharth wholehearted support. 'He was extremely mature. The first question I asked him was whether he would give me a free hand, and he was honest enough to tell me he had certain gaps in his experience and would want me to take charge. From that day, he has never intervened,' says Pahwa about Neeraj, who with his huge bank of knowledge continued to support Pahwa in the initiation process.

Eventually though, he stepped back, playing the role of a sounding board rather than getting involved in day to day management. The breakeven period was taking longer than expected for IVF and a lot of time had been wasted battling unwinnable conflicts with politicians and unions as a result of Meru's extant business model. Neeraj and the board left Siddharth and his team to fight these daily battles, whilst collectively devising a new line of attack to get the company back into shape.

The brand was still strong, and had managed to create a massive recall value in the cities in which it operated, but Gupta and the board realized that radical changes had to be made in the business model for the company to chart the course to profitability. One part of the problem was the external environment; the other was correcting the mistakes the company had made along the way.

One of those mistakes had been to not get out of the inventory led model quicker than they did. 'Meru started by wanting to emulate the Singapore model in India, and we perhaps took very long to realize that this is a different market with its own idiosyncrasies. We simply could not function like they did in Singapore or anywhere else in the world,' says Neeraj, mincing no words.

The 'Singapore model' in essence was the inventory led model, where the asset is owned, managed, and maintained by the cab company. In Singapore, this system worked faultlessly as the quality of drivers was excellent, the fear of and support from government with regard to tackling strife was instant, contrary to the antagonistic attitude of politicians in India towards businesses. Instances of accidents were lower and expenses on regular maintenance and repair were lesser.

Meru's experience in India turned out to be quite the opposite. The company had by this time put in a large upfront investment in buying a massive fleet of 5,500 cars. Possessing these assets not only meant dealing with breakdowns, accidents, heavy expenditure on maintenance and repair but also zero lack of accountability from drivers who would often get vindictive and damage cars if certain demands of theirs were not met.

'There were instances when drivers banged cars on an

electricity pole on purpose because they were not sanctioned a holiday,' remembers Gupta. And there were countless such incidents that the company had to put up with time and again.

Starting straight away with an asset light strategy would not have helped either. The efficiencies of this model could have been experienced only once an excellent service platform was established. Without creating a solid brand and an ecosystem—which meant proving to the consumer a track record on reliability, service etc, they would not have flocked to a technology platform, particularly in 2007 when there was no such precedent in India.

Anyhow, Meru's state of crisis meant that at no point in time could Meru have more than 70-80 percent of its fleet on the road. Ten days in a month would be lost either because a driver has taken-off without intimation, the car was in the garage after having met with an accident, or employees were striking. Owning an asset had become expensive and a hindrance to the smooth functioning of day to day business. Calls had to be rejected because a large number of cars would always be out of service.

The company slowly began fine-tuning its model in a bid to bring in greater efficiencies. There are three basic prototypes in the radio cabs business:

Ownership: Where assets are owned, managed, and maintained by the company. Drivers are not full-time employees with fixed salaries, but operate the cabs and pay a certain commission per day to the company.

Aggregation: An asset-light business model where the

operator does not own the cars, but focuses on the technology and backend to link cabbies with consumers by providing an online booking platform. The driver owns and maintains the asset and only pays a commission to be registered with the operator and benefit from their brand and technology.

Hybrid: A mix of ownership and aggregation where the asset is owned by the operator but maintained by the driver and eventually transferred in his/her name after a certain period.

It was decided that Meru would gradually start phasing out the first model entirely. Turning drivers into full-time entrepreneurs was the need of the hour. Getting them to own the vehicle would ensure that the drivers had an incentive to maintain it and take ownership of their actions. The company encouraged drivers to do just that. Meru would facilitate bank loans at low rates and the driver would be responsible for paying the EMIs. Meru got a reduced subscription amount as its commission, but its overheads also came down substantially. By early 2014, in a bid to get asset light, the company had managed to also get rid of 1500 odd vehicles from its 5,500 fleet, selling some and transferring others into the names of drivers if the vehicle was four years old. This brought in efficiencies immediately.

As the company shifted to this mixed—aggregation + hybrid—model, the focus was now on building a high-end IT platform making the business technology dependent, rather than asset reliant. This meant spending time on hardcore analytics, checking on consumer trends and patterns to predict the future requirements, devising offerings like a mobile App with an Insta-Pay option, card payment facilities, automated e-bills, trip tracker services for women safety etc.

The hard work soon paid off!

LOOKING INTO THE HORIZON

By early 2013 the combined efforts of Gupta, Pahwa and the rest of the management team started to pay off. The financials of the company were getting much stronger. Meru turned cash positive and was making profits at PBT level. Its margins were comparable to the spreads tech companies made and over the next 18 months it saw consistent improvement in the bottom-line to finally make a net profit—its holy grail—by 2014 on revenues of roughly Rs 600 cr. Meru by then had also become cash positive after servicing its debt.

The clear separation of the management and ownership had led to more accountability being fixed on performance and the focused action plan to tackle inefficiencies had yielded results.

Savings of Rs 6,000 were achieved per car only as a result of reduction in repairs and maintenance and better relations with the drivers. Meru also heavily lobbied with state transport authorities, and sought fare increases of between 10-25 percent between 2012 and 2014. A thorough qualitative and quantitative consumer analysis was carried out which showed that there were serious gaps in delivery. This was addressed by reducing cancellations from 10 percent to less than 0.5

percent. Quality control mechanisms were also put in place to address the issue of deteriorating cars. All of this ensured that the company was on the verge of making profits at the car level.

Meanwhile, innovation in business came with the launch of both Meru Plus for the premium consumer and Genie Cabs around mid-2013, a small, pocket friendly tourist cab service, catering to the mid-size mass market, charging customers for point to point intra-city travel. The first 50 vehicles were launched in Hyderabad on a pilot basis using a fleet of smart new hatchbacks like the Toyota Liva, Indica Vista, and Ford Figo. The idea with Genie was to introduce the middle-class, used to travelling in rickety rickshaws to a superior and safe travel experience at affordable rates. If Meru charged a tariff of Rs 22 per kilometer, the Genie ride was priced at Rs 16. The company could afford to keep price points lower because asset costs for the smaller hatchbacks were lesser and fuel efficiency was better.

Gupta reckons that Genie will capture 25 percent of Travel Link's revenue pie in the next five years as it expands to other cities like Pune, Delhi, and Bangalore and newer tier two markets such as Lucknow, Indore, Chandigarh, and Visakhapatnam over the course of the next few years. The plan is to commence operations across 20 cities in the next couple of years.

But what about a larger vision for the brand as a whole? Meru is on the cusp of an explosion in business, he insists, unfazed by the multitude of hold ups that have derailed the growth story of a company he so passionately built. 'We've come a long way in building the brand and creating the market, but in the larger scheme of things haven't even scratched the surface. This market is massive and there is tremendous scope for growth.'

It is difficult not to believe him when one takes a look at the numbers. Analysts peg the over Rs 10,000 cr Indian taxi market, including radio and tourist cabs at two million vehicles. Of this, 97 percent of the market is dominated by unorganized players. In the organized radio cabs segment of roughly 15,000 cars, Meru, Easy, and Mega Cabs hold 70 percent of the share, within which Meru is a market leader. The conservative estimate is that this market size will double in the next five years, which offers plenty of room for growth in the short run. The permit issue continues to remain a constraining factor but that is also slowly easing out as many state governments like Uttar Pradesh have been encouraging radio cab companies to launch services by issuing new licenses. Meanwhile, tier II towns are providing opportunities where prospects in metro towns have dimmed as a result of higher cost structures.

The test going forward though is not going to be battling the external environment so much, but building a better product and creating demand in newer geographies.

'Apart from Delhi, Calcutta, and Mumbai, the challenge with other cities is that there isn't an ingrained taxi culture. Our focus now will be to build that way of life, get people to move away from shared rickshaws and cycle rickshaws and convince them that taking an air-conditioned cab costs you the same,' Gupta says, referring specifically to Genie. He is confident that as standards of living improve and India urbanizes at a rapid pace his company will be standing-by with ready solutions to capture the opportunities. Given Meru's past track record in harnessing new markets like Hyderabad and Bangalore, where it built demand for intra-city commute from scratch, this shouldn't be too difficult say analysts watching the company.

While future plans are ambitious, they are rightly tempered down because of past experience in surviving an often hostile and unpredictable market. Having burnt cash initially in the inventory based model, the move to the hybrid aggregator model will ensure that capital expenditure on buying assets is curtailed in the future leaving a lot more on the table for operators says Gupta. Also the expansion of the cheaper hatchback version, Genie, into newer markets, unconstrained by the tariff regulations that apply to metered taxis, will broad base revenues.

Also, initiatives taken to improve utilization and leverage technology to perk up quality of service in the interim have already started yielding results. Meru has today scaled to a fleet of 8000 plus cabs, plying in six cities and serves over 1.8 million customers a day. Its call centre, where 400 staff work in three shifts, take 25,000 bookings a day and that number is only slated to increase. Gupta and his team have already set in motion plans to add ten more cities including Kolkata, Chandigarh, and Goa to its portfolio, and are confident that the company will show a compounded annual growth rate of 30 percent at least, for the next ten years. The long-term vision is to grow to 1,00,000 cars across the country by the year 2022.

'Even if we fall short of that target by half, 50,000 cars on the road with the assumption of five trips per car will mean 2.5 lakh transactions a day,' says Pahwa. 'Very few consumer brands do that kind of business daily.' The business has the potential to deliver a return on capital employed of 20 plus percent he adds. Critics who were skeptical about Meru's future too have come around given the marked improvement in the company's financial metrics.

Their confidence in the market and in the company's future, has also led India Value Fund, which post its seed investment of Rs 10 cr, ended up putting in another Rs 250 odd crore into the company to hold an 85 percent stake, to stay put in the business and wait for the right valuation before it cashes out. For a firm that has a typical investment horizon of five to seven years, IVF has already spent eight years at the helm of V-Link's affairs along with Gupta and looks at the association with pride and a sense of attachment about the enterprise. Nirula is confident that the efforts made at pioneering an entire segment in the Indian marketplace along with Gupta will result in stellar financial returns.

Gupta himself is tight lipped when quizzed about whether he'd like to cash out and sell his 15 percent stake in V-Link in the coming years, but insists that for him Meru is and will remain more than just another business venture, no matter what his future with the company. His only professional regret he says was the decision to dilute over 70 percent of the company. With hindsight he would have liked to retain 30 percent rather than 15 percent of the shareholding.

Whether or not he remains with the company, the thorough professional set up that's been established—entirely separating the functions of the board and the management—will guarantee a continuum in operations and make the ownership transition a seamless process as and when it happens.

And that perhaps will be the biggest testament to Neeraj's entrepreneurial character as he embarks on a new journey, toying with a new idea.

THE MERU ACADEMY

At 40, Neeraj has achieved what many can only dream of. He's made his millions, pioneered an entire sector and faced up to seemingly insurmountable challenges to emerge victorious. Having put a competent management team in place at Meru to look after the day to day affairs, he will now have a more hands off role in the company. But that doesn't mean he is hanging up his boots anytime soon.

Given how much more there is to achieve in terms of building a solid aggregation platform to capture a larger chunk of the market though, Neeraj is sure that the business will continue to excite him for a long time to come. But in the meantime new ideas continue to flash through his mind all the time, and he began laying the groundwork for one such in mid 2013.

That was the year he founded the Motor Education and Training Academy—an initiative to train and certify good quality drivers, who were equally Meru's biggest strength and its biggest failing. Gupta's struggle with drivers has been two pronged. One, because of the regulatory quagmire on the permit issue that made their availability scarce in markets like Mumbai, but also because the fight for good quality, well-mannered, safe drivers intensified as Meru expanded its fleet. The genesis of the problem of bad driving, he found was in the abysmal state of motor training schools in India. 'If you look at the motor training academies internationally, they are a class apart. Here, our driving schools are just agency schemes where you pay the money and get a license without actually being trained to drive.'

A quick study of the market for motor training schools showed Gupta that it was a hugely unorganized business with more than 3000 cars operating through 1500 schools in a city like Mumbai alone. Just like there was a crying need to organize the radio taxi business when Meru was launched in 2007, here too, the scope and need to convert this segment into an organized market was pressing. Capturing even a small share of the market in the country's top ten cities would change the game.

And so in affiliation with NSDC (National Skills Development Council), a pilot META training centre was launched in his old Goregaon office with the idea to provide standardized training on behavior, language, motoring skills, and knowledge of the latest technologies.

'We provide a very high-end platform with simulation, online training, certification, and placement services. I've yet again tried to do what I started out doing a decade and a half ago at the garage—value add and organize the driving schools market into a more professional set up,' says Neeraj, explaining the concept.

He is confident that this initiative will become profitable quickly as it gains critical mass, but importantly, he looks at it as a way of giving back to a trade that made him the man he is today. It has also given him a chance to spend more time with Farhat, who quit her job and did an advanced driver training course from the UK to join Neeraj in the venture. Needless to add that it also has positive synergies with Meru's core business, given the desperate need for good quality chauffeurs needed to go along with its swanky taxis.

After years of roughing it out in a space where he spent a significant amount of time staving off brute elements, Gupta says he enjoys the pace of work which is more relaxed and less demanding. He likes to spend free time thinking of new business ideas—a nascent retail venture called Freshkins, which comprises physical, mobile, and web stores, selling perishables like fruits and vegetables has just been launched—painting, and clicking pictures, hobbies he couldn't find time for when he was building Meru. His home is proof of how seriously he takes these passions, packed as it is with impressive art work, frescos and interiors that have been personally supervised by him.

While restless by nature and always seeking to explore newer pastures, money and riches don't excite Neeraj a great deal any longer. Not merely because he's already made a considerable amount, but also because at heart his needs aren't very flashy. He told a journalist once that his dream was to retire to a small farm house away from the city, create a menagerie, own a horse, and paint. He stands by that.

But that plan is still a long way into the future. For the moment the unflinching focus, as a key shareholder in V-Link, is on getting Meru into top gear and sustaining the leadership position as the market explodes and newer players make a beeline. It is also to make Motor Education and Training Academy India's leading training school by consolidating the fractured market.

'My vision is to have a bulk of India's drivers come to META to get themselves certified. I'd like to see it become a benchmark for quality training and a pre-requisite for anyone wanting to drive a car in India,' says Gupta reflectively, pondering over the question for a bit.

He has age on his side and a long road ahead of him to prove what he is really worth. The past decade has only been a teaser of what an easy-going, unimposing, suburban lad from Mumbai, equipped with a sharp acumen, and quiet drive to rise above the ordinary could do to make his life extraordinary.

His real journey is only just beginning—with and beyond Meru.

THE EMAMIWALLAHS

RADHESHYAM GOENKA AND RADHESHYAM AGARWAL - EMAMI GROUP

The mass migration of the Marwaris from Rajasthan began under the reign of the British East India Company. As transport and communication became easier, with the railways linking the remotest parts of India, it quickened pace in the mid-nineteenth century, when Rajasthan saw an exodus of sorts. Shekhawati traders and businessmen who had established their empires for centuries in the harsh desert state as money lenders, shop keepers, traders of commodities like opium and cotton and financiers of the royals, began their voyages to presidency towns across India—Hyderabad, Mumbai, Mysore, and Calcutta.

Here they became agents of the British, brokers in the colonial trade and suppliers of key commodities—textiles,

References 1-15 taken from Maheshwari Arun's *Ek Aur Brahmand*. New Delhi. Radhakrishna Prakashan Pvt Ltd.

tea, jute, precious metals, and spices for export to Europe. They flourished a good deal in the city of Calcutta, which served as the capital of British India until 1911. It was in the labyrinthine alleys or *pattys* of Burrabazar, adjacent to the Hooghly river in Central Calcutta, that the community made its first millions—setting up shops to trade in yarn and textiles, hitting the big league in the opium trade and in Burrabazar's cloth markets that spawned the empires of the Birlas, the Goenkas, the Kedias, the Singhanias, the Neotias, and a dozen others.

Burrabazar is today a large, chaotic wholesale market, a relic of times gone by in the glitz of the new economy. But one can still get anything, if willing to pay the right price for it here. It's recent past has been plagued with records of towering infernos, soaring crime graphs, and petty gangsters running *satta* rackets and *hawala* scams in its crowded by-lanes. Not stories of ingenuity and enterprise. But it continues to remain a thriving commercial hub for thousands of merchants and hawkers. Its winding, congested *pattys* christened after the products they sell are choked with carts, goods carriers and throngs of cyclists carrying wares for sale across the city. Steel and scrap, gems and jewelry, garments and textiles, fruit and vegetables are all traded here, sitting in *gaddis* just like they were a century ago.

But the inevitable smell of decay for anything that's been standing too long is all pervasive. The new generation wants to stay far away from the heat and dust of this uncouth trading outpost.

When Banshilal Kandoi left Bikaner to experience the hustle and bustle of this flourishing thoroughfare in the 1940s though, things were different. Burrabazar was a goldmine of opportunity.

BIKANER TO BURRABAZAR

No sooner had Banshilal set foot in Calcutta, he started earning money like a magnet draws metal. Starting by dabbling in paint trading, Kandoi was soon engaged in an array of businesses—from hardware and cosmetics, to stationary and general trading. He bought up no less than 5 *gaddis* in premium commercial centers of Burrabazar like *Khangra Patty* and Armenian Street[1].

J.C. Law was the only manufacturer of pencils in India back then and Kandoi became its all India agent, and in a matter of few years, one of the wealthiest Marwaris in Calcutta. The J.C. pencils were known more for their brittleness than for how they wrote, but Kandoi's agency enjoyed a roaring monopoly as import of pencils was banned.

Soon enough though, as import restrictions were lifted, the fragility of J.C. Law's pencil also broke Kandoi's financial muscle. A wrong gamble by his brother in silver speculation accelerated his downfall. His rise in the Calcutta society had proved to be ephemeral and the riches and affluence vanished as quickly as they had appeared. Kandoi's palatial house was first to go and with creditors knocking on the doors every day, soon all but one *gaddi* in *Khangra Patty* remained.

The family moved into a very modest rented house.

It was in these punishing circumstances—that saw his father go from soaring prosperity to crippling adversity that Radheshyam Agrawal, was growing up.

Agarwal was born in the princely state of Bikaner, now famous for its sweets and snacks, two years before India got her independence, but moved to Calcutta at the age of five. He was one among four brothers and five sisters and studied at Burrabazar's Maheshwari Vidyalaya, one of the oldest schools founded by the Maheshwari community in Calcutta. Despite being anything but studious, more engrossed as he was in cricket and football, whose teams he captained in school, academically Radheshyam was a brilliant student with a photogenic memory. He always stood first despite bunking lectures, much to the bewilderment of his principal Ram Mahesh Chaubey.

'Do you have some magic wand?' Chaubey would ask, as Radheshyam topped his class every year. His wayward nature concealed the effort the boy made, spending hours pouring over his books on the rooftop in the glaring afternoon heat. He would need to read his text only once for it to get imprinted in his memory for ever.

As I met him in his relatively modest, but tastefully done-up two story apartment in Kolkata's leafy Southern Avenue, overlooking the lakes, it happened to be Agarwal's 69th birthday. And, as if to prove a point about his sharp memory, he delivered at full volume line after line from Napoleon Hill's iconic 1937 book *Think and Grow Rich* and Dale

Carnegie's equally popular *How to Win Friends and Influence People*, which he first read 50 years ago. These books became his bible and the practical wisdom in them his guiding light in business through the years.

Agarwal's intellectual prowess always exceeded text book knowledge. From essay writing to oratory and debate, he was a school whiz kid. An external jury once invited to judge a debating competition in Maheshwari Vidyalaya were so impressed with his debating skills that they gave him the first prize even with him having flagrantly broken all the rules of the game[2].

It was in the same school that Agarwal also met his namesake and life companion Radheshyam Goenka. Better attestation of the cliché that opposites attract cannot perhaps be found anyplace than in the thick friendship that the duo formed. If Agarwal is boisterous, aggressive, a go-getter and a visionary, Goenka is shy, soft spoken, and impossibly reticent. The former is in your face, media savvy, a great marketer and still full of ideas, the latter is the diligent executor, the numbers man willing to take a step back, and remain behind the scenes.

Goenka's family had migrated from faraway Churu in Rajasthan—the gateway to the Thar desert. His father, Keshardeo, made a name for himself in the bullion market of *Tisibara* and later became a member of the Calcutta Stock Exchange, where he'd operate till he passed away. He would become the biggest driving force initially in forging the enduring partnership between the two Radheshyams.

It was in class five that Goenka joined Maheshwari Vidyalaya. He was one year junior to Agarwal. A common friend of the duo, Hariram Poddar, who also happened to be Goenka's neighbour and Agarwal's classmate had introduced the two. They hit it off instantly and Agarwal soon started visiting Goenka's home more or less on a daily basis to tutor his junior on the school syllabus. Keshardeo's temper and obsession with discipline were legendary and kept the other Goenka children on tenterhooks. But for the Radheshyam duo, he had nothing but affection. He held a special soft corner for his son's friend and would feed him fresh *kachoris* which he loved to make himself.

In 1964, Agarwal passed his B.Com degree and went on to pursue Chartered Accountancy, which he finished at the first attempt and with Merit. Goenka completed his B.Com a year later, and went on to pursue M.Com and L.L.B. Belligerent by nature, Agarwal too decided he needed to hone his legal acumen and joined Goenka to do law. When Emami was formed, Goenka would look after sales and finance, while Agarwal the chartered accountant would be the marketing and advertising brain. This duel split in responsibility was decided as per each one's area of interest.

St. Xavier's College, where Agarwal had enrolled to do his bachelors, was then a snooty college for convent educated kids of the rich. Burrabazar kids from Hindi medium schools went to City College. But Agarwal was bent on breaking this tradition. He polished up his English with rigor and ensured he got a seat at Xavier's. The crowd there didn't accept the coarse Marwari lad with broken English initially.

'I had no wealth, no status, and no personality, but I could make anybody smile. I became popular in class because of my wit,' he says. The college principal, Father Juris was so stunned at the confidence with which Agarwal, despite his language inadequacy, delivered an extempore performance in a competition, that he made him the class representative.

Goenka, meanwhile chose City College in the neighborhood like other Marwari kids in those days. He has little memory of college, he says, except that he was an average student with not much of a flair for academics.

'Also, I didn't have the requisite marks to get into Xavier's,' says Goenka.

'How could you, with me as your teacher?' retorts Agarwal.

It is my first brief introduction to the friendly squabbles the two indulge in every so often. They've been friends for 60 years and one often completes the other's sentence. By 1968, the duo had finished their education. Their real learning however, had begun many years earlier.

FRIENDS TO BUSINESS PARTNERS

His dramatic financial ruin had taken such a toll on Banshilal Kandoi's mental health that the man fell into a deep depression. By 1955 he had lost pretty much everything and so deep in crisis was young Radheshyam Agarwal's family that ancestral jewelry had to be pawned to make ends meet. The one shop in *Khangra Patty* that the family retained was now being looked after by Bajrang, Agarwal's elder brother who had left school midway to join his father's once booming trade[3].

Agarwal, with his friend Geonka in hand, would rush to the shop straight after school to help Bajrang. It is here, long before they mastered law or chartered accountancy that the duo began their lessons on debit and credit, soaking in as much practical knowledge about the tricks of the trade as they could. 'We learnt how to keep creditors happy even when there was no money to pay them, to deal with difficult customers, to collect payments, to manage inventory and stocking, to spend conscientiously,' says Goenka.

Bajrang would inevitably vanish when creditors came to collect their payments in the evening, and it was this young duo who were left to deal with their wrath[4].

'We'd keep them engaged in long gossip sessions, serve them tea and *kachoris* and just as they were about to leave, slowly let slip that Bajrang had the money and wouldn't be back till tomorrow. The next day we'd repeat the same exercise,' chuckles Agarwal. 'But we never swindled them. Even though there were delays, the payments were always made.'

'Call it karma if you may, but we faced the same music when we started out,' laughs Goenka. The business partnership between the two was a seamless transition from the fun and frolic that they engaged in as children in Bajrang's shop. They began to think seriously on the lines of collaborating while in college itself.

The motivation was not some brilliant idea that had

struck them. 'We were more worried about how we will meet everyday once college finished,' says Goenka.

Trading of goods didn't interest either, given how low the margins were. And so, while still in college, the duo would spend hours in the second hand bookshops at College Street pouring over books that contained chemical formulas for cosmetics. Their plan was to manufacture such products which they noticed were selling like hot cakes in Burrabazar[5].

Agarwal and Goenka soon began dabbling in numerous businesses even before finishing college. From repackaging *Isabgol* and tooth brushes to trading in the famous Jaisore combs to manufacturing board games like Ludo, for which Agarwal would prepare low-cost, homemade glue and sit himself with workers to paste the boards, they tried their hand at a number of things. Despite being busy with the demanding college schedules, the duo would lug their goods on hand pulled richshaws, selling from shop to shop in Burrabazar.

Goenka, being better placed financially was also separately occupied in another partnership, with one Revtilal Shah, a son of his father's old friend, who had broken new ground at the time, developing India's first indigenous home automation technology. Shah and Goenka had almost inked a deal with the Calcutta Municipal Corporation to supply automatic switches, but the proposal was expensive and so it never took off. Goenka subsequently also tried his hand at manufacturing steering wheels for Hindustan Motors, but that venture also failed. He was destined to do business with his old friend Agarwal.

But lack of capital always constrained their ideas and

success continued to elude the duo as money was always in short supply. Their struggle continued for almost three years before they realized that without adequate seed funding their trade wouldn't flourish. And here's where Goenka's father Keshardeo came to their rescue.

The generous patriarch gifted them a princely sum of Rs 20,000—a handsome amount in those days and forged a 50:50 partnership between his son and his friend. That is how Kemco Chemicals was born. It was a gesture of kindness Agarwal still cannot forget. It was as if a messiah had descended down to alter his wretched fortune.

KEMCO CHEMICALS

Kemco's beginnings in business coincided with the start of a decade of deep political turmoil and an irreparable decline in Bengal's industrial fortunes.

The 1967 state elections saw the United Front, chiefly propped up by the CPI(M), form the government. A year later the Naxalbari peasant uprising led by hardliner CPI(M) leaders like Charu Majumdar and Kanu Sanyal broke out and by 1969 it seemed like the communists had firmed up their reign in the state. Better part of the next decade saw large scale violence in a bid to crush the Naxal movement. The state was put under president's rule in 1970 itself and by 1975 Indira Gandhi had declared nationwide emergency. A period of political stability returned only by 1977, with the beginning of the Jyoti Basu era. But Basu is credited also for presiding over Bengal's dramatic industrial decline, leaving the eastern state, as many called it, an industrial wasteland by the 2000s.

The state's marquee turn of century manufacturing units, which were already precariously poised by the 1960s, had begun to go into terminal decline by the 70s. They were unable to compete in the new market and were being severely mismanaged, which led to prominent pharmaceutical companies like Bengal Chemicals and a dozen others either being nationalized or shuttered down by the time Basu became Chief Minister[6].

It was in such bedlam that Kemco Chemicals was incorporated, with much confidence around Diwali 1968. Operations began with a small manufacturing unit at 48, Muktaram Babu Street in the vicinity of the palatial Marble Palace in North Calcutta. The Rs 20,000 lifeline that Keshardeo had extended to Goenka and Agarwal had boosted their spirits, and even while the environment around them was anything but ebullient, it was such adversity—that threatened to put many age old companies out of business—that would provide them with their biggest opportunity a decade later—the buyout of Himani in 1978.

The early days though were anything but smooth. Within a year of founding Kemco Chemicals, Goenka and Agarwal saw their capital being completely wiped out. The business ran on credit and as luck would have it, customers conned them even without their knowing it. 'The biggest lesson from this setback was the need to keep proper accounts. We'd do our daily calculations but never keep a tally, and that did us in,' says Goenka.

Shamefaced and filled with remorse, the duo went back to Keshardeo to tell him they wanted to wind up. But he thundered at the mere suggestion and told them he was willing to give them Rs 1 lakh more, but there was no question of running away[7].

And so, with their animal spirits reignited and better judgment of how to approach things, the duo got back into business. Kemco Chemicals saw considerable success between 1968 and 1978. To begin with, the company started repackaging cheap cosmetics like Bulbul and Kanti Snow, Pomade or the poor man's Vaseline—products that had great patronage in the nascent cosmetics market of the country. But margins were low and the duo would sell full cartons to wholesalers in Burrabazar for as little as Rs 36 a gross or Rs 3 a dozen.

A couple of years passed, but Kemco's expansion was chugging along at snail's pace. Around this time both Agarwal and Goenka also got married—to Usha and Saroj respectively, and with that came added responsibilities. The pressure to make more money was mounting and so when an opportunity came to work for Calcutta's then premier corporate house—the Birla Group, the two couldn't let it pass.

Goenka would go on to head of the income tax department at the K. K. Birla Group and Agarwal would become Vice President of the Aditya Birla Group by the time they had resigned five years later. Both had a spectacular run with their respective divisions, but it is Agarwal's stint, as narrated by Arun Maheshwari in his Hindi biography of Radheshyam Agarwal '*Ek Aur Bramhand*,' that makes for an incredible story.

The man with 'a ladylike' voice, Madhav Prasad Birla, as Agarwal remembers him, rejected him not once but twice, merely because Agarwal didn't have the good looks and personality that MP looked for in candidates that came in to interview for positions.

As Maheshwari recounts in the book, in the first instance an assistant to the company's president P.D. Daga interviewed Agarwal. He was so stunned at the remarkable quality of this not-so-promising looking candidate's Hindi and English essay writing test, that he accused Agarwal of having mugged up his answers.

'But you just gave me the topic,' protested Agarwal.

He was taken to meet MP in any case, who intently gazed at him for a while.

'Have you passed your C.A.?' he asked in Marwari.

'Yes,' replied Agarwal.

'And B.Com?' questioned MP.

Agarwal stood motionless, taken aback at the question. How could he have passed C.A. without having done his B.Com, he thought to himself. He didn't answer.

'Can you knot a tie?' continued MP.

Agarwal remained silent.

He was rejected. 'Babu wants real personality,' Daga informed him as he stood outside waiting to hear the decision.

The affront got even more humiliating the next time

Agarwal went for the interview at the behest of his good friend K.M Mimani. 'Will you go to Zambia?' MP asked, when Mimani had categorically told him that Agarwal will not leave the city. He was made to wait for nearly an hour and a half before being cast off yet again on another flimsy ground.

But the young man got third time lucky. It was as if he was destined to work for the Birlas. This time the interview call had come from the Aditya Birla Group, and it didn't take long for Agarwal to make an impression as he answered tough technical questions on accounting principles with élan. He was brought on board on a measly salary of Rs 800.

It didn't take time for Agarwal to rise up the ranks at the Birla Group. No sooner had he joined, Agarwal brought about dramatic changes in the group's accounting practices in the face of stiff resistance from employees. It came to his notice one day that that staff in the finance department were being paid overtime charges because the balance sheet would take six to eight months to be prepared after the financial year closed on 31 March, and the department would be struggling to file tax returns on time. He began looking into the issue and it became clear to him that two reasons—the time taken to evaluate fixed assets and audit the debtors—were delaying the entire exercise as everything else would be ready on time.

When he pointed this out to the company's president Mr Bathwal, and told him he could close the balance sheet one month before the financial year ended if minor changes were brought about, Bathwal dismissed his suggestions as laughable. Every other big company in the country was doing the same thing Bathwal told him. 'Were they mad?!'

Not the one to give up so easily though, Agarwal pursued the matter. He prepared a 250 page report to prove his case and handed it over to the company's auditor P.M. Narialwala. When the affair reached 'Aditya Babu's' doorstep, Agarwal told him he would hand in his resignation if he couldn't prove himself right.

The affair created quite a stir across company subdivisions and Agarwal even became a subject of ridicule as people waited for him to falter with his experiment. Succeed, he did eventually, and handed in the balance sheet to be signed by Birla much before the financial year closed. Even then, some officers, and self proclaimed experts in the company bent on proving him wrong nitpicked on every little mistake Radheshyam had made. It didn't dent his spirit. For every mistake they'd point out, he would come back with four blunders they had made in their own balance sheets. Birla was mighty impressed and soon began sending Agarwal to company offices across the country to give lectures on this new method he had devised.

Agarwal introduced a string of other best practices in the group during his stint. Several departments were being run inefficiently and Birla didn't have it in his nature to run a microscope over every decision. Agarwal, true to his meticulous *baniya* nature, sought to change that approach. So, when he realized that the company was overpaying its decades old insurance provider for an erroneous policy, he immediately confronted the company and sought better terms. Similarly at annual group conventions he would openly question fallacious claims made by company presidents on divisional performance.

Birla knew he had found a jewel and Agarwal would go on to become the young scion's closest confidant by the time he decided to resign five years later.

Kemco by then was thriving, bringing in a turnover of Rs 70,000 annually with the launch of brand Emami in 1974. Goenka and Agarwal were doing day jobs and then managing the factory in the evenings, but soon enough the work load was getting too intense. Around this time Birla, thoroughly taken in by Agarwal's acumen and integrity had also decided to make him the President of his company Hindustan Gas Limited. But tempting as the offer was, Agarwal knew it was time to make one choice—either become a full time businessman or spend his life working for someone else.

And so, RS, as Birla would call Agarwal, walked into his cabin one day, after the decision to make him president was announced, with a resignation letter in hand. 'I don't want to betray you Aditya Babu, by quitting three months down the line, so please accept this.'

Birla refused to accept it making all possible effort to convince Agarwal to stay on. Realizing however that RS was firm about his decision, he relented, but requested him to come to office just once a week with no change in his salary or designation. Agarwal couldn't rebuff his mentor and so agreed to the offer reluctantly, but would never encash the cheques that Birla sent him at the end of every month. Their association and friendship continued right till the latter's untimely death in 1995[8].

Meanwhile real traction was building up in their own business after a six-year long struggle between 1968 and 1974. Being voracious readers and now also exposed to the workings of a large corporate set up like the Birla Group, Goenka and Agarwal soon realized that if they were to enter the big league they would have to differentiate on the product line, think out of the box and improve their margins. There was no alternative to it in a hugely crowded market consisting of a myriad of unorganized competitors, all offering the same kind of products.

In those days there was a craze for imported cosmetics and foreign sounding brand names. Under the License Raj there was a ban on such discretionary items, but a big latent demand for them nevertheless. Most people couldn't afford the imported versions because of a 140 percent excise duty that they carried.

The duo decided to cash in on this opportunity and launched brand Emami. 'It didn't mean anything but sounded Italian,' says Goenka. The cold cream, vanishing cream, and talcum powder they launched under the new brand got such a tremendous response from the market that it took no time for Emami to get established as a household name. There were a couple of things they did right, points out Goenka.

Kemco didn't have a penny to spend on grand advertising and promotional activities like its rivals Pond's and HUL.

So instead what it did was sold old wine in a new bottle. It revamped the packaging entirely. In those days talcum powders would be sold in tin containers with the brand name directly screen printed on the tin. There was nothing attractive about it. Emami instead, introduced for the first time in the Indian market, blow molded plastic containers with photo tone labels. The beautiful ivory colored container with golden labeling looked like it had been shipped from abroad.

The fact that the Indian government at that time didn't mandate an M.R.P (Maximum Retail Price) to be printed on the container helped them tremendously. Such a hit was their product—particularly the talc—that shop keepers would be scrambling to keep it in stock. 'If Ponds gave them a 10 percent retail margin, our talcum powder would fetch them spreads of up to 400 percent because people thought the product was imported,' says Geonka.

Goenka's brother Rajkumar, who now looks after the perfumes division of the brand, narrates an interesting anecdote. As a young boy, when he took the first batch of twelve Emami talcum powders to be sold in Calcutta's Bagdi Market and quoted a price of Rs 60 a dozen, the owner of Maheshwari Stores almost threw him out. 'You think you are now the owner of Nycil that you are quoting such a price?' he asked Rajkumar in Hindi. 'Just keep it for a day Malik, along with our toothbrushes,' the boy pleaded to him.

Barely a day later 'Malik' sent for Rajkumar and asked for another batch. The product was flying off the shelves and within three-four days several other retailers in the vicinity were asking for it. 'So much so that a batch of twelve that was sold for Rs 60 in Bagdi market was selling for Rs 30-Rs 40 a *dabba* in New Market' recalls Rajkumar. Do bear in mind that this was the time when most of Kemco's other products were being sold at barely Rs 3 a dozen.

This sudden spurt of demand created a panic back at the factory. Emami had printed barely 3000 labels having never anticipated that the talc would be such a raging success. Pannalal Jhawar, the owner of Calcutta Labels had used a high quality Japanese paper for the labeling and so when Goenka and Agarwal went back to him with an order for another 10,000 labels, he was dumbstruck. He had run out of the paper and it would take a minimum of three months for the import consignment to come he told them.

'He gave us another label which looked similar but wouldn't stick to the board. So what we did was got the workers to paste it on each and every container and hold it tight for 15 seconds so that it would stick,' chuckles Rajkumar. 'It was worth the effort. In a matter of four days we had swung the company around from a loss of Rs 20,000 to a profit of Rs 5,000 a day. Had we waited longer, perhaps we would have lost the opportunity.'

Goenka and Agarwal had soon mastered the art of overcoming the restrictions placed by the license Raj through their own ingenuity. Emami's success stunned the biggies in the market like HUL, who Rajkumar says, made discreet enquiries on how blow molding was done. One of their company representatives even came down to Emami's nondescript factory to get a glimpse of what this new upstart of a brand had up its sleeve.

The company's other products also similarly gained traction. 'The vanishing cream gave Ponds neck-to-neck competition within months and our market share went up to 25 percent in a couple of years making us market leaders in the segment. Our cold cream sachets were also a big hit,' says Agarwal.

This early success taught the duo invaluable lessons on the importance of branding and packaging, areas that would form the core of Emami's success in later years.

THE BIG LEAP

K.L. Roy, the manager of United Bank of India and one of Emami's bankers was mighty impressed by its improving performance. One day, around 1978, Roy asked Goenka and Agarwal to come down and meet him. 'There is a sick cosmetics unit that's breathing its last. Will you be interested in buying it?' he asked.

Roy was talking about Himani Ltd, a company owned and run by two brothers A.R. and S.R. Banerjee who couldn't see eye-to-eye. Its products—Himani Snow and Himani Glycerin Soap were well known in West Bengal and it had a large, well laid-out factory in North Calcutta's Belgharia suburb. But there were problems galore at the factory, and it was bleeding heavily. Agarwal and Goenka's ears perked up. The brand was already well established in the eastern parts of the country, and if there was merely a problem with how the factory was being run, they could perhaps salvage its fortunes they thought.

'What would it cost?' Agarwal asked

'Rs 8-9 Lakhs,' said Roy.

Emami by this time had a healthy balance sheet, but there was no way the duo could have raised so much money. While there was a clear opportunity waiting to be pounced on, the financial risk involved was considerable given the many difficulties that Himani was mired in.

'How much are you able to offer?' asked Roy.

'We have roughly Rs 2 lakhs which we can spare.'

'Pay the rest of the amount in installments then,' Roy said, desperate to clinch the deal and get the burden off his back[9].

And so, Himani had a new owner by 1978. It was the first in a string of acquisitions that Agarwal and Goenka would do through the course of the next few decades.

It didn't take more than two years to turn Himani around and make it stand on its own two feet. The Banerjee brothers were retained in managerial positions despite the lack of any apparent need for their services only in order to show workers, who would usually be wary of new owners, that their jobs were safe. The Banerjees embodied the lazy, smug Bhadralok character of Bengal's erstwhile aristocracy. Even as the enterprising Marwaris, who had their backs against the walls, were busy seizing control of all trade and business in the state, the Bengali gentry were squandering away the massive fortunes their forefathers had earned during the colonial times—on merry drinking sessions, women, and a debauched lifestyle.

In a generation, the Bengali factory owner was almost threatened to extinction as the community's faux Marxist insularity coupled with an air of conceit about their pedigree and the glories of days bygone left them far behind in the race.

'The beauty of the Bengali,' says Agarwal mockingly, 'is in his contentment to work for someone else. Give him a car, a chamber, a modest salary, and call him *babu* and that's it, he is a happy man.' The Banerjees evidently were kept 'happy' and would promptly leave the factory at 1:30 pm in the afternoon, calling it a day.

Agarwal and Goenka meanwhile were toiling day and night in a bid to get things back on track. Himani was in tatters and their first mission was to cut down on unnecessary costs. So a fleet of eight-ten company cars that the previous owners had bought, with no justification for the cost but to up their snob value, were promptly disposed off. A detailed assessment was carried out in every department to study what was going wrong where. Agarwal and Goenka spent the first few months micromanaging every aspect of the business, so much so that Agarwal in a bid to improve the quality and shine of Himani's glycerin soap, would sit with workers for hours teaching them how to polish it.

'They started calling it R.S. polish in a few days,' he recounts.

Customer relationships and marketing activities were also improved and slowly but steadily Himani started making money.

The duo laid out grand plans for the company. They had a strong pulse of the market and soon realized that Borolin Antiseptic Cream manufactured by J. D. Pharmaceuticals was a very popular product in the market and enjoyed a virtual monopoly. Their trade sources had indicated to them that they were not happy with the company as the product would always been in short supply, and particularly so during the winters.

Soon it was decided that Himani would launch an antiseptic cream in direct competition to Borolin and would call it Boroplus. Borolin, despite being in the market for 50 years, had seen no innovation in its packaging or brand identity and was still sold in the tired, worn-out avatar in which it was launched half a century ago. It was decided that in order to stand out, Boroplus would be packaged in colorful plastic tubes accompanied by an advertising blitz on the radio.

By 1984, Boroplus was put on shelves and would prove to become Emami's first big success at the national level. A strike at Borolin's factory around the same time gave Agarwal and Goenka just the push needed for a new brand to make place for itself, and it wasn't long before Boroplus would become the market leader, establishing itself as India's Ayurvedic antiseptic cream of choice. Along with all the brand extensions including a moisturizing lotion and a prickly heat powder, the 'Boroplus range' is today a Rs 400-500 cr brand.

Only a year after the launch of Boroplus though, in 1985, Himani had to face up to its biggest challenge—reining in the trade unionism that had started to cripple its smooth operations.

The company didn't have a large workforce, but it did have a large number of temporary workers and that was a trigger for the charismatic politician—labour leader of the day Ajay Ghoshal—to set off an agitation at the Himani plant. Ghoshal was then a much feared leader, so Goenka and Agarwal made every attempt to settle the issue with him amicably. He would walk into negotiations fashionably late, holding up the duo for two-three hours on every occasion.

Agarwal in particular, with his short temper and lack of patience for too much nonsense lost his cool on one occasion after Ghoshal hadn't turned up for a meeting two hours past the decided time. Goenka and Agarwal drove off the factory premises telling workers that if their *neta* was going to behave in such a manner they were not interested in negotiating further.

Ghoshal reached the scene soon after the duo had left, and was fuming. He quickly mobilized workers to *gherao* the two Banerjee brothers. Word was sent to Goenka and Agarwal about the agitation, but they didn't budge. If they gave in to his demands this time, there would be no end to them they thought and declared a lock out at the factory which lasted nearly two months[10].

Workers were steadily losing patience with Ghosal's unreasonable tactics, having soon entered a state of financial distress. They approached Agarwal and Goenka, pleading with them to have one last meeting with Ghoshal. The duo refused point blank, telling workers there was no need for a third party union leader to sit on the negotiating table when the solutions were going to be provided by the two of them.

'*Gherao* his car when he comes to the factory, don't let him get off. Chase him away,' Agarwal told a worker leader who had come to meet him. 'Only then will we have a meeting.' Goenka and Agarwal had turned the tables on Ghosal, using the very *gherao* routine he and other labour activists used, to coerce factory owners to yield to their demands. Soon enough he disappeared from the scene, leaving the management and workers to thrash out a compromise.

This was the second and last labour agitation in the history of Emami's near 50 year existence. Agarwal and Goenka had tackled a similar attempt to unionize workers at the 48, Muktaram Babu Street unit as well a few years earlier, by instituting a workers committee with whom Agarwal would sit every month to sort out issues related to wages, working conditions, working hours etc. He took workers into confidence with his inspiring speeches and oratory and told them that he was willing to listen to all their demands, but wouldn't tolerate unionization at any cost. All decisions would be jointly taken in committee meetings every month and all reasonable demands would be met.

'*Agarwalji* would pinpoint at trouble makers during these committee meetings,' remembers Goenka. '"Kamal, what mischief are you up to these days?" he would roar away'. Rabble-rousers like Kamal would be publicly dealt with in every meeting, which guaranteed that in a few years only workers who had serious concerns would come forward and make their case. Very often the workers did have legitimate issues about how certain divisions in the company was functioning, but equally their demands would also be politically instigated on many an occasion. Agarwal and Goenka had devised a clever strategy to sift the legitimate from the unreasonable.

The Worker's Committee is in existence till date as an arbitration forum between workers and the management, despite Emami's scale and operations having grown multifold. The company employs 20,000 workers and the fact that there haven't been labor troubles at any of its facilities in the past four decades in either a unionized state like West Bengal or elsewhere in the country, is evidence of the fact that Goenka and Agarwal have been successful in instituting a well functioning, democratic set up to resolve prickly labour disputes that are any industry's nemesis.

BRAND IT LIKE EMAMI

By the mid-eighties there was no stopping the Emami gravy train. Over the course of the next three decades, Goenka and Agarwal thundered through one successful product launch after another, and Emami became among India's flagship homegrown FMCG brands. It was as if luck was chasing the two Radheshyams. They had the Midas touch.

A year after Boroplus Antiseptic Cream, Boroplus Prickly Heat Powder was launched in 1983. Mentho Plus Balm followed in 1987, Navratna Oil in 1989 and Sona Chandi Chyawanprash a decade later. Having started with low cost, low quality cosmetics manufacturing at their shed in 48, Muktaram Babu Street, Kemco Chemicals became a public limited company by the mid 90s, with its shares listed on the Bombay Stock Exchange under the name Emami Ltd in 1995. Three years later Himani was merged into this listed entity and also rechristened as Emami Ltd. When the company went in for a public issue of shares a decade later in 2005, it was oversubscribed within seconds by 36 times and has since given stellar returns to investors, increasing shareholder value by a whopping 1600 percent.

Goenka and Agarwal's uncanny ability to spot niches, create strong brand differentiation and aggressively promote their products has been at the core of Emami's success. 2005, apart from being the period when the company came out with its IPO was also the year Emami created branding history of sorts by launching the first ever fairness cream for men—Fair and Handsome. There were no players in the men's skin whitening segment and it gave the company a big first-mover advantage, even though me-too products launched by other companies like HUL, Garnier, and Nivea jumped the bandwagon very quickly.

Goenka and Agarwal kept their ears close to the ground and had discovered that 30-35 percent of fairness cream users were men. It was Mohan, Goenka's son, who first brought home the idea after a visit to Andhra Pradesh, where he witnessed intense demand from men for Fair and Lovely tubes. There was clearly a massive suppressed market waiting to be exploited and without further ado a detailed project report was prepared to expeditiously launch a product. With Shahrukh Khan brought in as its brand Ambassador, Emami had no difficulty in creating this category from scratch, where it is today the segment leader with an over 50 percent share of the near Rs 400 cr market.

In fact no facet of Emami's business can tell the tale of its evolution better than the branding and marketing ingenuity Goenka and Agarwal applied to every product they launched in the market. They pioneered several unique concepts which have now become the norm.

In 1980 superstar Rajesh Khanna strode through screens across India becoming Chief of Emami in the film *Agar Tum Na Hote*. Product placement has become an all important branding tool today, but that was an era when in-film advertising was unheard of. It paid rich dividends. Emami was on the verge of becoming a household name, but wasn't yet known widely. Khanna's oblique endorsement of the company gave Emami widespread exposure. The company also became the exclusive sponsor for *Vikram Aur Betaal*, a hugely popular TV program on Doordarshan. It was done to bail out Ramanand Sagar, an old friend of the Radheshyams who was on the verge of bankruptcy. But the mythological program's popularity gave Emami a presence in every household as its ads played before and during the interval. The Emami jingle too was on everyone's lips ever since it was first heard on the radio in the 1970s.

Goenka and Agarwal continually harnessed star power to give their brands a large reach—from Hema Malini to Amitabh Bachchan, Rekha, Shahrukh Khan, Bipasha Basu, Kareena Kapoor, Priety Zinta, and Madhuri Dixit to cricketers like M.S. Dhoni, and Sachin Tendulkar to even Pt Birju Maharaj, over 60 celebrities have been faces of one or the other Emami product through the years. Madhuri Dixit signed an eleven year contract with the company at the peak of her career and an exclusive 'Beauty Secrets by Madhuri' range was also launched in 2002.

Today, the company spends nearly Rs 300 cr on advertising and promotions annually as a result of this celebrity fixation. That's roughly 16 percent of revenues, a figure greater than most other players in the FMCG sector. Often one brand is endorsed by as many as five-six celebrities and the company has found new ways to incorporate their presence in order to stop a celebrity fatigue from setting in.

While Emami sent Salman Khan's production house a legal notice initially for using 'Zandu Balm' in the song '*Munni Badnam hui*' without their consent, they eventually began using the song for their own benefit as a product promotion tool. 'Celebrities give a brand instant recognition. While they may not be as effective as they were in the past, they've definitely worked for us,' says Agarwal.

But Emami's marketing tactics go beyond merely splashing film stars across hoardings he says. From using photo tone rather than screen printing in the initial days to introducing plastic moulds in place of tin containers, snazzy packaging has been an important ingredient of the success of Emami's products.

After establishing Boroplus, Emami replicated the same strategy when it introduced Navratna Cool Oil in 1989. It isn't that there weren't other local manufacturers of this product, but Emami standardized it and instantly made it recognizable with the catchy *'thanda thanda, cool cool'* tagline.

When Sona Chandi Chyawanprash was launched, real gold and silver dust was used to differentiate the product from those already being sold in the market. Agarwal and Goenka even promised anyone who could prove that there was no real gold and silver in it that they would be given 1 kg of gold free[11]. In days when the buy-one, get-one free ploy was still unknown, Emami started an innovative promotion tactic by giving free hair clips with their vanishing cream, much to the wonder of rival brands like Ponds. Free sampling was another trick Goenka and Agarwal used long before everybody else did.

Despite a battery of brand managers and advisers, the duo still retain the final word on branding and have even deferred launches at the nth moment if they remained unconvinced about a product's brand identity.

Ayurveda always played a big part in Emami's brand positioning right from the beginning. The company chalked out a strategy to promote the use of this ancient medicinal system by developing a distinctive Ayurvedic identity for several of its products. From neem, babool and clove to honey aloe vera, saffron and turmeric, the use of herbal and traditional ingredients in Emami brands and brand extensions helped Goenka and Agarwal cater to a wide market beyond India's urban populace.

It was the duo's personal interest in promoting Ayurveda that propelled them to make use of this ancient science in their business. People like Kaviraj Hari Shankar Sharma the former dean of the Gujarat Ayurveda University at Jamnagar was their family friend and hours spent with him understanding the preeminence of this primordial medicine fuelled their curiosity about the subject. The Himani Ayurveda Science Foundation patronized by the duo became engaged in constant innovation and is today an integral part of Emami's R&D ecosystem.

'You can sell Pizza in Timbuktu, but not in Jhumri Telaiya, unless you add the local flavor to it,' says Agarwal explaining how his company captured the idiosyncrasies of the Indian market by customizing products to suit local tastes.

Emami's biggest triumph has been its ability to combine a traditional knowledge base with modern manufacturing and packaging techniques, which helped it stay relevant in an increasingly competitive market. Alongside its focus on tradition, over the years, the duo also hired the best of expertise in the world of branding and advertising to create a distinct niche for itself and evolve with times. Alyque Padamsee became its consultant way back in the 80s. Ashok Kurien as well as Babu Datta, who worked on L'Oréal's brand identity, were also roped in at different points in time when the company needed a makeover. Today the man who advises Apple on its advertising strategy also counsels Emami on how it must approach branding.

'Seven pillars make or kill a brand,' says Goenka.

'Packaging, pricing, product, promotion, distribution, advertising, and margins to retailers. We ensure there is equal focus on all these aspects.'

Along with the seven pillars, a tight control on costs and a business model that focuses on tapping only niche markets with low competitive intensity, low penetration and high margins ensured that Emami continually outperformed sectoral growth. Over 70 percent of its revenues come from power brands such as Boroplus, Zandu Balm, Fair and Handsome, and Navratna and there has been strong emphasis on consolidating their leadership position in these categories even while growing other segments.

In the recent years Emami has given added impetus to improving its distribution channels to reach consumers across markets particularly in the rural areas through what it called its 'Project Swadesh' which was unveiled in 2010. Goenka and Agarwal forged tie-ups with ITC's e-Choupal and Kisan Seva Kendras for instance, where they did not have a presence, super stockist networks across important states, and increased their product coverage through direct distribution micro channels like vans.

By 2013 the company had 3000 distributors, 5,600 sub distributors and 6 lakh direct retail outlets across 8,200 villages making its products available in more than 40 lakh stores according to the company's annual report. With 250 products in its fold, Emami Ltd today has a market presence in 60 countries with operations of its first greenfield international unit also having begun in Bangladesh. This success has largely been as a result of organic expansion.

But in 2008 Goenka and Agarwal made a big audacious move to embark on a long arduous mission to acquire Zandu Pharmaceuticals—one of India's best known manufacturers of balms and OTC medicines. It was a grand takeover battle full of suspense and intrigue that exemplified the fearless risk taking capacity of this duo. Because even as the world was plunging into a protracted financial crisis, and global stock markets were in a virtual tailspin, the duo were busy battling it out with the owners of Zandu, to seize control of the 100 year old balm manufacturer.

Here's how the story unfolded.

THE ZANDU TAKEOVER

Named after Mahatma Zandu Bhattji, the son of Vaidya Vithal Bhattji, who was a personal physician to Ranmal, the then King of Jamnagar, Zandu began operations in 1864, on a small piece of land on the bank of the Rangamati river in Gujarat. Jam Sahib, the prince of Jamnagar had bestowed this gift upon Mahatma Zandu after he impressed the royal with his accurate diagnosis and deep study of Ayurveda.

As demand from the market for Zandu's products grew, it was decided by 1919 that more money needed to be raised for its expansion and hence the company was taken public. Zandu's good run continued unabated and by 1936 it had put up more factories at Vapi, Sanjan, Silvasa, as well as Ankleshwer in Western India to make bulk drugs and intermediates.

But the insular, non-savvy approach of its management stymied the company's growth in the later years. Ownership battles and a worn-out administration unable to catch up with the times had missed seizing the opportunity to participate in India's booming FMCG sector post liberalization. Zandu's revenues were steadily dwindling year after year.

Nonetheless, some of its brands were still going strong even by the turn of the century. Zandu Balm, Zandu Chyawanprash, Zandu Kesari Jeevan, Zandu Pancharishta, Nityam Churna etc, were among its most prominent offerings. So when Agarwal's son, Harsh, was approached one day by a broker to pick up some of Zandu's shares that were trading hands in the secondary market, he studied the proposal very carefully[12].

What he found was that there were huge synergies between Emami and Zandu in the various categories in which the two operated. There was also tremendous underlying brand potential that wasn't being marketed properly and it took only a cursory study of the balance sheet for Harsh to understand that the Rs 200 cr market cap company was hugely undervalued. It had zero debt, considerable amount of real estate and a strong play in the Ayurvedic OTC space which, if fused with Emami's dynamic distribution, packaging and branding prowess could create a powerhouse of a company.

Harsh was keyed up. Emami had been on the prowl for such an opportunity for a long time, but nothing exciting had come its way. He shared his findings with his father and 'Goenka uncle' with a view to initiate an unsolicited bid to buyout Zandu. The two gave him all their support.

The months post this decision to pursue the acquisition, are what legendary boardroom battles are made of. Nearly 24 percent of Zandu was controlled by the Vaidya siblings—a brother-sister duo, who couldn't see eye to eye. They were decedents of Jugatram Vaidya, Zandu Bhattji's grandson who took the company's reins and expanded it after his grandfather's passing.

The Parikhs—a gigantic Gujarat based joint family were co-promoters of Zandu, with the largest shareholding of 33 percent. The Parikh patriarch had been an accountant with Zandu and had gradually seized control of it from its original promoters, the Vaidyas. A cluster of other shareholders owned the balance 39.48 percent of the company, while 3.9 percent was in the open market.

Devkumar Vaidya and his sister Anita were interested in selling out, and Harsh engaged with the duo immediately. But their personal animosity delayed negotiations indefinitely. Emami had already acquired a minority stake of 3.9 percent through the open market to demonstrate its interest, but the constant back and forth between the Vaidyas on the most minor issues led to a considerable holdup in its bid to buy out the duo's 24 percent stake. It took between September 2007 and May 2008 for the company to finally complete the acquisition, for which Emami paid Rs 130 cr or Rs 6,900 per share.

As a 27 percent shareholder in Zandu now, it was incumbent upon Emami to make an open offer for another 20 percent stake in the company, as per the Takeover Code rules in the country. Once Emami made a public announcement to this effect, it set the stage for a battle royale with the Parikhs.

Through their lawyers, the Parikhs instantaneously alleged violation of SEBI's takeover regulations and argued that they had the first right of refusal over Vaidyas' decision to sell their shares. They also alleged that Devkumar Vaidya, being an invitee to board meetings of Zandu, was an insider privy to price sensitive information and was thus barred from dealing in Zandu securities without prior approval from the company.

Within four days of Emami announcing its open offer, the Zandu board also sent a notice to the Bombay Stock Exchange to discuss a preferential allotment to the promoters in a bid to reduce Emami's stake. Emami responded summarily stating that as a large shareholder of Zandu its consent was needed before a preferential allotment was done. Independent directors of Zandu were also opposed to such a move by its management.

In the meanwhile the matter went to SEBI, which transferred it to the Company Law Board (CLB). The Parikhs decided to take the legal route rather than sitting on the negotiating table with Emami, and moved the Bombay High court. Agarwal, who along with his son was the key negotiator in this deal, had several meetings with the Parikhs, giving them three options to choose from—sell their shares to Emami, buy Emami's stake or agree to work as partners. Neither of these options were palatable to the Parikhs, who didn't quite get along with one another and didn't agree on anything. At one point, it looked as if things had hit a dead end.

Luckily for Emami, the Parikhs couldn't prove their ROFR (right of first refusal) in the courts, while the CLB dismissed a petition filed by Zandu with regards to the Takeover Code violations and insider trading charges, leaving the two parties to settle the matter outside the courts.

By September 2008, SEBI cleared Emami's open offer as well, leaving the Parikhs with no option but to enter talks for a settlement. Parikhs agreed to sell 18.18 percent of their stake in Zandu to Emami at a price of Rs 15,000 plus a non-compete fee of Rs 1,500 per equity share. Emami also acquired through open market purchases another 28.5 percent, taking its total stake in Zandu to near 71 percent. All of this took the overall acquisition cost of the deal to a whopping Rs 730 cr.

It was an audacious deal to put it mildly. The market was convinced that Emami, with a turnover of little under Rs 600 Cr, was paying too much for Zandu. Even youngsters within the family including Harsh, who was the key force behind the takeover, had apprehensions about shelling out this kind of money, considering that the conclusion of the deal also coincided with the beginnings of the global meltdown that had its genesis in the US subprime mortgage crisis.

'Both ICICI bank and the State Bank of India had sanctioned the loan, but pulled out at the last minute,' remembers Goenka. 'A day before we were to make the payment to the Parikhs, we were left high and dry.' The crisis was ultimately averted at the last minute, but Agarwal was unmoved by these setbacks. He had support from a person whose opinion mattered to him the most and several well wishers and friends in the banking circles from whom money could be mobilized. 'When everyone stood in opposition, Goenka told me they couldn't foresee what I could,' he says with a smile. He could prevail over his sons and other family members only because Goenka—his better half in business stood steadfast by his judgment.

Today, the results are there for everyone to see. With the acquisition of Zandu, Emami now has one of the strongest Ayurvedic brands in its portfolio with a segment leadership in the balms and chyvanprash catagory. Zandu saw revenue growth at the rate of 27 percent in 2012, outperforming the Emami corporate average. Its health care division gave it access to the OTC and ethical business segment, including a portfolio of 140 health solutions. This is pegged to be a growth driver for the Emami in the medium term. The acquisition created value for the shareholders of both companies and also increased Zandu's profitability considerably. Emami Ltd is today Rs 1700 cr brand and Zandu contributes Rs 500 cr or 22 percent in turnover to that pie. Its market capitalization too has grown to Rs 10,000 cr odd from barely Rs 1250 cr when Zandu was acquired.

For a company that had earnings of barely Rs 150 cr in 2007, the turnaround has been remarkable. 'It took years of concerted effort to align marketing, sales, and procurement functions of both companies to drive synergies, improve brand visibility and make Zandu's products available on Emami's distribution channels,' says Naresh Bhansali, the Chief Financial Officer of the company. Skeptics who believed that Emami had overpaid for Zandu were proven wrong.

Barely two years after the Zandu acquisition, Goenka and Agarwal were back in the headlines again for their efforts to acquire Paras Pharmaceuticals. This was an even bigger gamble as Emami had put in a bid for an eye-popping Rs 3,400 cr. They lost out in the end to British consumer goods giant Reckitt Benckiser, despite being the highest bidders. Agarwal is still mystified by how that could have happened and is certain that some mischief happened in London where the deal was sealed.

Ever since, the duo have been slow when it comes to M&A activity in the flagship FMCG business. But that is only because such opportunities are few and far in between. 'We are constantly evaluating options. But the valuations need to be correct and we need to see if an acquisition will really bring in the desired synergies,' says Agarwal. 'It is difficult to find a right match because there are very few companies that meet our expectations and those that do, are unwilling to sell, given how well the sector is doing.'

EMAMI—THE DIVERSIFIED CONGLOMORATE

Even while Goenka and Agarwal were busy expanding their FMCG portfolio, the duo never rested on their laurels. They were ceaselessly on the lookout for new business ideas in sectors that had untapped potential. It is no surprise then that from newsprint to real estate to ball pen tip manufacturing, edible oil, retail, pharmaceuticals, cement, and biodiesel, the duo, over 40 years managed to grow their footprint not just in the consumer goods space, but across diversified categories. In many of these businesses Emami has also come to enjoy a leadership position.

Emami Paper Mills is the largest manufacturer of newsprint in India at present and CRI Limited is the fourth largest ball pen tips manufacturer in the world. FMCG contributes only a third of Emami's revenues today, while a chunk of its Rs 6000 cr group turnover comes from these myriad companies. In fact the edible oils division has a larger turnover (over Rs 3,000 cr) than the flagship FMCG vertical, even though the latter is more profitable.

There has been a perennial debate on whether diversification is a good business strategy. There are those that believe focus is a key to success, while others who argue that diversification helps large conglomerates spread their risk. Agarwal has his own theory. 'There are no related or unrelated businesses,' he says. 'Indian companies are still miniscule in size when compared to their global peers, and until they reach a certain scale, all areas of opportunity must be seized.'

The partners followed this simple logic every time an opportunity to enter a new line of business came their way. Their approach was simple—they took hold of companies in doldrums at dead cheap valuations and worked towards quickly turning them around. 'M&A is in their DNA,' says one Emami associate. 'They are the archetypal serial entrepreneurs, though very few people now recognize this fact.'

It is true. From Himani in the early days to Frank Ross, which is perhaps the oldest pharmacy chain in India that was about to shut shop when they bought it and now has 150 outlets all over India, to CRI Limited which was born in the shuttered workshops of an ailing American cash register machine manufacturer, to the large format leisure retail venture Starmark, Goenka and Agarwal have scripted numerous terrific turnaround stories.

And where a business was losing too much money even after they did everything they could to salvage it, they cut their losses and got out as quickly as possible without waiting for it to turn the corner. So, when the duo realized two and a half years into their venture to manufacture monofilament lines that there was excess capacity in the market and very little margin to be made, they swiftly got out. Similarly, when their steel casting business failed to take off after a series of misadventures, they sold it off at a minor loss.

'I use the same strategy in my business today—cut losses and move on,' says H.M. Marda of Chandramukhi Implex, an old friend of the duo from the Birla days, who helped them set up numerous businesses including the monofilament lines factory in the seventies.

Agarwal and Geonka saw their first big success outside the FMCG space when the paper mill was set up in Balasore, 195 kms north of Bhubaneswar in Orissa in 1982. Having worked for the Birla Brothers, Agarwal had observed at close quarters the running of the various plants of Orient Paper Mills and was interested in exploring whether Emami could set up a paper making facility as well[13]. 'The per capita consumption of paper was amongst the lowest in India and after a detailed project study we realized that this business had a very promising future. We decided to throw in the dice,' says Geonka.

And so in 1982, production began with machinery that had capacity to make 10 tons of paper per day. Not many people had hopes that the duo would succeed in this line of work. Contrary to accepted wisdom, they had decided to purchase second hand machinery from Europe to commence operations. By merely changing a few bearings and bushes, these machines could run as efficiently as new ones and cost only a quarter of the price. But this was reason enough for skeptics to write obituaries even before the plant began operations[14].

Goenka and Agarwal quickly proved their skeptics wrong. The machines worked flawlessly and the factory began operations with the frantic whir of engines. The duo had decided to let operations be completely professionally managed from day one and put a fantastic team of technical experts and engineers to the task. But there were problems galore. From floods that inundated the factory every monsoon to treating toxic effluents that needed to be discharged into the river, the first year was spent battling numerous odds.

But in due course, the operating environment improved.

New machinery was added and production steadily went up. Since demand for newsprint was tremendous, it was decided that instead of printing paper, newsprint would be produced at Balasore. Growth also happened inorganically when the sick Gulmohar Mills in Dakshineshwar was acquired in 1994.

What started as a small unit manufacturing 10 tons of paper a day, eventually became a Rs 500 cr company by 2013, and is today a gigantic division of the group that has an installed capacity of 1,45,000 tonnes per annum. Emami Paper Mills' clients include all the marquee newspaper brands of the country as well as government presses, banks etc.

Real estate was another sector that always caught Goenka and Agarwal's fancy for its ability to give very high returns. Many of the sick units the duo had acquired through Emami's history came with vast tracts of land. And even if some of these businesses had failed to take off after the acquisition, the value of their real estate yielded extraordinary profits for Emami always. The monofilament lines business for instance never managed to make money, but the factory in which it began operations was an ailing unit of Banjo Chemicals located in Kolkata's Picnic Gardens neighborhood. Emami still owns the land which is today worth crores of rupees.

Similarly with Zandu, when everyone was unconvinced about the high valuations Emami was paying, the duo was confident that the company was worth much more than what they had offered because of the massive 2.5 acre land parcel Zandu owned in Mumbai's prime Dadar area. Today Zandu Realty, an Emami Group firm has developed the property in collaboration with Sheth Developers, keeping half the area for itself and monetizing the rest.

Goenka and Agarwal had plunged into real estate fully by 2006 itself, right in the peak of the boom, buying up land banks across the country from Jhansi to Coimbatore and Hyderabad to Kolkata. Among one of their iconic projects has been the 25 lakh sq ft Emami City, built on 15 acres of land that the company had managed to acquire from an ailing public sector aluminum factory on Jessore Road near the airport. Located near the new lake town, it has become an emblem of Kolkata's regeneration.

It took several years however for the duo to firm up their decision to enter the real estate business in a full-fledged manner. Before Emami Realty was set up, the company had dabbled in the sector, but only as financiers or minority partners. Interestingly Agarwal's curiosity about the segment was triggered off after he had to forcibly recover some money he had lent to a company called Deluxe Builders back in 1986. As luck would have it, the owners turned out to be crooks and wouldn't return Agarwal's cash, which compelled him to foreclose some of their properties in Calcutta's prime locations. He lost heavily, but the incident gave him a taste for the business[15].

Since then Emami worked in affiliation with several partners such as the Orbit Group and built iconic Kolkata landmarks such as South City Complex on Prince Anwar Shah Road. But the duo decided to remain in the shadows because it was a space that thrived on black money and illegitimate funding. Goenka and Agarwal didn't want to affect Emami's brand image, and neither were they interested in doing underhand dealings.

It was only when there was a cleanup in realty dealings around 2007 that they decided to come to the forefront. 'We will not get into businesses where the dealings are not clean, no matter how big the opportunity. That has been and will remain our philosophy throughout,' says Goenka who is now keen to position Emami more aggressively as a real estate brand.

The duo gave up opportunities to branch out into various other segments like mining, power generation etc in the 2000s, taking a conscious decision not to enter any business where they would have direct and constant interface with the government. It is no fluke then that the company has steered clear of all controversies when several big corporate houses in India are battling allegations of crony capitalism and corruption.

Non-controversial in business, but an indignity of another kind that would be the true litmus test of their character was in store for the two friends in 2011. The AMRI fire set their lives ablaze.

FLAMES OF WRATH

The horrific memories are still fresh in their minds. And an uncomfortable silence engulfs the room as I gently probe. 'Tell me about AMRI. What happened?,' I ask, as the two shift gaze towards one another with a melancholic gleam in their eyes.

'It was perhaps the sins of our past lives that we were paying for,' says Agarwal, after a long pause. 'Who knows, it could have been an accident, maybe even sabotage. Whatever it was, it changed our lives forever.'

Ninety-three of the 164 patients—men, women, children admitted at the Advance Medical Research Institute in South Kolkata's Dhakuria area were virtually gassed to death after a fire in the hospital's basement sent poisonous smoke gushing through its central air-conditioning vaults. The state of the art facility co-owned by the Shrachi group and Emami had no outlet for fumes to escape and the fire brigade reached only an hour and half later, by which time the damage was done. Press reports spoke of obvious lapses in safety and there was all-round outrage with headlines flashing news of a rapidly increasing death toll as India's worst hospital fire tragedy shook Goenka and Agarwal out of their sleep on that dreadful morning of 9 December, 2011.

The sheer magnitude of the catastrophe was unimaginable. Neither Goenka nor Agarwal looked into day to day operations of AMRI and rarely if ever attended any of its meetings. But allegations of neglect flew fast and thick. The press raised questions about lax regulation and profiteering at the cost of safety. Toxic materials stored in the basement ultimately caused the fire according to authorities, while fire alarms did not work either. As directors on its Board and 66 percent owners, the duo couldn't escape blame and the harsh media gaze that followed.

'It was like being in Hitler's gas chambers,' the papers

quoted victims as saying, perceptibly livid at hospital authorities and staff, who they claimed had fled the scene, leaving patients to suffocate to death, while the building was being gutted down. The West Bengal government swiftly cancelled AMRI's license, ordering a police investigation in the days that followed. What followed were the worst four months of Goenka and Agarwal's yet unblemished life.

Criminal charges were slapped against six members of the family on the board of AMRI, which included Goenka and Agarwal, Goenka's son Manish and nephew Prashant and Agarwal's daughter Priti Sureka and son Aditya. Sureka and Aditya absconded from the scene and nobody knew of their whereabouts, while Agarwal was remanded to judicial custody and admitted into a general hospital ward after he complained of heart problems. Goenka, Manish, and Prashant were arrested and jailed along with the chairman of Shrachi, S.K. Todi and his son Ravi.

From a life of dazzling affluence to the confines of a small cell in a Kolkata jail, Goenka saw the experience bringing about a radical transformation in himself overnight. He spent four months in police custody and 14 days in jail, before being granted bail. The thirteen hours between 5 am and 6 pm that he'd be restricted to his small cell every day, he read the Ramayana and the Ramcharitmanas. He slept on the floors at night and ate jail food. And to his own surprise he got used to this life of austerity. 'My conscience was clear. I knew I hadn't done anything wrong and so did my inmates from whom there was tremendous sympathy. But it changed the direction of my life.'

Goenka no longer felt the same zeal for business and mentally withdrew myself from the humdrum of material life to delve into deeper questions at the spiritual plain. He was always pious, having inherited a deep sense of severity from his mother, who was an ascetic and a devout pilgrim. 'I never had much love for money, but post AMRI, I decided to consciously cut down on my needs. I own an Audi today only at the insistence of my children. I wanted to sell it off and buy a Maruti Ertiga whose advertisement I'd seen in the papers while in jail. But my kids wouldn't let me,' he complains.

Agarwal, meanwhile, stunned everyone with his jolly as ever attitude. He would be cracking jokes with others in the SSKM hospital ward much to his wife Usha's surprise. Goenka was extremely worried about his friend because of his heart ailment, but Agarwal had left it to fate, not bothered by the crippling circumstances in which he found himself. His conscience too was clear, heartbroken as he was by the tragedy that had unfolded in a hospital he had ironically taken over to serve mankind.

The sorrow of having lost so many innocent lives in their hospital still lingers on, and the case is in courts today. But neither Goenka nor Agarwal worry about their fate. God will decide they say.

ALL IN THE FAMILY

At 36, Harsh, Agarwal's son holds the demeanor of a suave corporate tycoon. He rarely smiles, broods over every question with a solemn weightiness and is evidently itchy when asked tricky questions he'd rather keep for another day.

'*Ye dekho hamare prince aa gaye*,' Agarwal says teasingly, as Harsh walks into the room on the day of our interview, to touch his father's feet before leaving for work. Must I take the 'prince' reference as a hint to who will succeed the patriarch from the Agarwal side? The two friends—Agarwal and Goenka— have been giving finishing touches to a succession plan since 2011 and there have been whispers that one son from each of the families will finally take over the reins from their respective fathers as next chairmen of Emami. The names doing the rounds are those of Harsh and Goenka's elder son Mohan. Harsh refuses to confirm anything, only saying that the current structure of the company lets the next generation function with ample creativity, initiative, and autonomy for each member of the family handling a division to continue implementing his or her own vision, without having to worry about succession.

Eight members of Goenka's family including his sons, brothers, and their sons and six members of Agarwal's family including of his sons, a nephew, daughter Priti, and her husband Raj occupy various managerial positions across the Emami group today.

'We all started out very early,' remembers Harsh. 'We'd be made to sit in Saturday meetings where strategy and acquisition ideas were discussed and my father would plunk heavy international magazines on our laps asking us to spot trends and ideas. I remember going to the market to learn the ropes with our sales people right after tenth standard,' he says. Each of the Agarwal and Goenka kids went through such initiation programs before they were absorbed in the company and rose through the ranks to their current positions.

The current configuration of Emami has each of the siblings handling different divisions. Harsh, Priti, and Mohan look after various aspects of the flagship FMCG business as directors on the board. Aditya Agarwal and Manish Goenka, the younger sons and thick friends just like their fathers, take care of the edible oil, newsprint, and hospital verticals. Nephew Prashant who was instrumental in growing Emami's exports business, handles international operations while Agarwal's son-in-law Raj looks after real estate.

At a time when high decibel succession battles and family splits have hogged headlines where India's biggest corporate empires are concerned, Harsh is all too aware of the lofty challenge in front of him and his siblings in keeping the herd together. But he is confident that Emami will thrive because each member of the family understands that their strength lies in working together rather than as separate entities. Preserving harmony and taking that extra effort to let the larger good prevail over personal ego clashes is a legacy the clan has inherited from its two founders. In fact while single families have been unable to stay together, this unrelated (by blood) clan has gone as far as to mull a change in their surnames to a common Emamiwallah to have a more cohesive identity.

'Just like in a marriage, in a joint business too there needs to be mutual compromise. We treat our relationships with each other with the same sanctity as we treat marriage,' says Harsh. The fact that in tandem with a growing clan, the group too has expanded to newer areas, makes accepting these generational changes easier. There is work for everyone with responsibilities clearly defined. Moreover a stringent family council, governance, and remuneration committees as well as a trust managing Emami's shareholding have been set up that limits rights of individuals. This restricts authority to take decisions that might be disruptive for the overall organization.

Outsiders might find this arrangement stifling, but Harsh says this prescriptive-rules based structure works for them. Everything from remuneration, to what kind of car one can own to the kind of companies they can invest in (liquor manufacturing, hotels are out of bounds) have been cemented in a formal code of conduct to avoid any covetousness and distrust from creeping in. A family council meets every fifteen days, where decisions are taken with mutual consent. Everything—right from jewelry for the wives to shares in the company are divided equally.

At a personal level, the two families lunch together in office, spend weekends at each others' homes and haven't missed their annual holiday together for years now. Agarwal and Goenka infused a culture of egalitarianism among family members years ago, when they'd travel to different parts of the country on work. What Goenka would buy for his wife Saroj, he'd buy for Agarwal's wife Usha and the wifes of their brothers. And vice versa. This easy logic has been extrapolated into Emami's governance structure as well, no matter that the company is now a multi-national entity worth thousands of crores.

Blending a brand of idiosyncratic traditional wisdom that's alive only in Indian family businesses perhaps, Emami has also made a concerted effort over the years to professionalize the set up to keep itself in sync with the latest corporate governance norms. While there might be no clear separation between ownership and management, full-time chief executive officers of finance, strategy, and business development, separate CEOs for R&D, sales, supply chain and human capital as well as operations along with several independent directors and advisors form the core of Emami's management team.

'Yes, department heads do tend to get superseded, and roles, though well defined theoretically, tend to overlap sometimes,' says an employee wishing to remain anonymous. 'However, the overall work culture is great. It isn't an impersonal company. I feel a deeper connect, because at Emami, we value personal relationships that a sterile corporate environment does not.'

'The chairmen often enquire about things like whether I am saving enough money for the future, or expects me to be present at a religious function at their residence. That might seem intrusive for some, but I cherish it because it gives me the sense that my employer cares for me beyond work,' admits another employee, at a managerial level. 'Not many chairmen with 20,000 employees under their fold would waste their time building such a personal rapport.'

Agarwal and Goenka themselves are instantly dismissive

of any suggestion that good corporate governance is akin to a transition to complete professional control devoid of an environment that harnesses personal relationships. 'If that were the case, why did Wall Street banks fail?' asks Agarwal. 'Do so-called professionally managed companies give their investors the kind of returns we do? Can they claim to be better managed?'

It is a valid point and talking to analysts, one gets a sense that the duo have managed to strike that fine balance between managing the aspirations of their family on one hand, and a changing business landscape that demands more accountability on the other. Harsh likes to dwell more on the strengths of a family run entity—quicker decision-making, more nimbleness and agility in changing processes, higher risk taking capacity and more room for maneuver, unconstrained by the rule books—than on its shortcomings. It is under his and Mohan's initiative after all that Emami scripted two of its biggest success stories of the recent past—the Zandu acquisition and the launch of Fair & Handsome, a category creator. These successes are proof, possibly of the Emami Gen-X's conviction that business growth and family ownership need not necessarily be mutually exclusive goals.

Moreover the AMRI incident has only reinforced the importance of continuing together. Had it not been for their collective strength, the fire incident had the potential to cripple business operations, employee morale and the individual lives of those from the family implicated in the case.

Nonetheless, it will be difficult say observers, for the

second generation to maintain the same level of respect, admiration and uncanny synchronization of ideas and ideals that led Emami's two founders to such incredible heights. Most research shows family businesses disintegrating after three generations. Goenka and Agarwal, however, are unperturbed by such statistics. 'We've done what we could, the rest god will take care of. Why worry about the future?' asks Goenka philosophically.

Seeing the love that continues to flow between the two families, it is easy to appreciate why the duo are so undaunted.

THE ASETICS

The Hindu way of life has had a profound impact on both Goenka and Agarwal. The former is more avowedly devout than the latter, deeply engaged for years in imbibing the teachings of Sri Sri Ravi Shankar and the Shankaracharya. Like his mother, who gave up all worldly possessions and would travel third-class with pilgrims to different parts of the country, Goenka too, puts himself through the test of living a life of rigor. He wakes up at 3:30 am and spends the next two hours performing an elaborate Puja, keeps regular fasts, and undertakes journeys to holy sites like the Kumbh mela every so often, where he becomes one among the thousands of devotees, leading a life devoid of comfort. The more well-off he has became, the simpler his needs have gotten.

Agarwal, meanwhile, calls himself an atheist, but only half-jokingly one supposes, given how seeped he is in the Hindu tradition, with a sprawling *mandir* right outside his bedroom. And the grasp he holds over ancient texts is incredible. 'Money is the root of all evils,' says this capitalist, 'if not accompanied by a divine wisdom to put it to good use.'

'*Kuch log Lakshmi ko maa samajhte hai, kuch log bhogya*,' he tells me, lapsing into Hindi. 'And if you think of *Lakshmi* as *bhogya*, a resource for luxury, women, laziness, tyranny etc, you will go to hell.'

Both founders today play the role of mentors at Emami—sounding boards for the big decisions that their children take and advisors in their separate areas of expertise. They've withdrawn from day-to-day goings-on, but don't envisage complete retirement. They like to set short, medium and long-term goals for the company and say they are confident that in the next three-five years, the group will double turnover and profits and triple capital expenditure. Agarwal says he wants to see Emami Ltd's market capitalization go from roughly Rs 10,000 cr to Rs 30,000 cr in five years.

'But what got me till here, will not get me till there,' he says, telling me about his mantra, which is to get the company to constantly adapt to change by studying the shifting dynamics of business.

Friends amaze at their success. 'I hadn't in my wildest dreams ever thought they'd reach such soaring heights,' says Marda, the old friend and colleague from Birla days. 'They were always progressive and acted keeping the future in mind. Sometimes it backfired too because they were ahead of their times—like the instance where we started a food processing unit, manufacturing coated peanuts and rice crackers. But most often they've got it right, and I am confident the future will be no different.'

Goenka and Agarwal say they'd like to see Emami recognized as a large conglomerate in the future, not merely a consumer products company. They have undertaken heavy expansion in areas like cement and healthcare and harbor no doubts that over the next few years people's perception of their brand will evolve too.

They will do it their own way as they always have—blending the traditional strengths of family and relatives, and a microscopic control over little aspects of their trade with new age business practices that have become integral to the survival of any globalized company.

From a small cottage industry at 48, Muktaram Babu Street, in the heart of old Calcutta, to a sprawling new corporate headquarters at Emami Tower, dotted with brilliant works of Hussain, Raza, Souza, Bikash Bhattachajee, Shekhar Roy, Chattrapati Dutta and others, Emami's story encapsulates the evolution of the humble *baniya*. His ability to adapt, adjust and change with the times, without losing that distinctive spirit of enterprise that is his truest identity.

Goenka and Agarwal are worthy inheritors of this heritage. But it is their incredible personal journey and the story of their eternal friendship that's stuff of legends. They don't make them like these anymore!

THE ONLINE BANIYA

Rohit Bansal - Snapdeal.com

Not so long ago, a wife in Nashik would await her husband's trip to Kolkata, so he could pick up Dhaka cotton saris for her. A mother in Indore, would look forward to her daughter's arrival from Bangalore, for a slab of special Mysore Sandal Soap. Kids in Sangli passed time, waiting for their uncle and aunt to return from overseas to be able to devour foreign chocolate, and teenagers in Aurangabad would anxiously count days so they could head out to Mumbai, Delhi, or Chennai during the vacations to pick up branded shoes, watches, perfume, or sunglasses.

And then in the late 2000s it all began to change. The wife, the mother, the kid, and the adolescent needed no longer to play the waiting game. All it took to buy what wasn't locally available was the press of a 'buy now' button on an e-commerce website. They linked you to the handloom shop in Kolkata, the Cauvery store in Bangalore, to vendors of chocolate, mobile phones, or shoes in Delhi and Mumbai.

A network of sellers—from specialty boutique stores in obscure towns to high street brand names and luxury goods chains in the metros as well as fledgling entrepreneurs in tier two cities—were instantly connected to a speckled group of buyers across the country. Supply reached demand and vice versa, creating a virtuous business cycle, spinning a whole new web of enterprise that came to be known as e-tailing.

As per one estimate, 25 to 30 million Indians have today transacted goods and services worth $2.5-$3 billion online, with the average consumer basket growing by 50-80 per cent. And this is just the beginning. India, say analysts, is on the cusp of an e-commerce revolution that will see the industry grow to $70-80 billion by 2020.

Many a starry-eyed entrepreneur made a beeline to partake in this furious growth, but today, only a few have lived to tell the tale. Dozens have shut shop and no less than 70 percent are expected to meet the same fate sooner, rather than later, reckons one investor. It is survival of the fittest here, and among one of those, who has not only survived, but thrived in this dangerously tricky terrain, providing a beacon to India's ecommerce narrative is Rohit Bansal, who along with his childhood buddy, Kunal Bahl, founded Snapdeal.com in 2010.

His company, Rohit claims, is India's largest e-commerce marketplace and provides a platform to 50,000 merchants and growing. One out of every six internet user is its member and customers in 4000 plus towns and cities in India buy/

sell products on his website which has in barely four years of its existence, come to command a third of the market share. With $350 million raised in several rounds of private equity funding from marquee investors, including global giant e-bay, it is today hitting $1 billion in sales.

This remarkable story though was at the threat of never being written.

THE DILEMMA

In 2009, two years into his entrepreneurial outing, Rohit Bansal faced the classic dilemma most failed, hungry entrepreneurs do—dump the idea and go back to the cushy job that would pay for a car, house and 'stability', or stay put, and give it another shot. Live to see one more day of disillusionment and failure perhaps, but lean on the optimism that eventually somewhere something has got to give.

It wasn't an easy choice. All the angel funding Rohit and Kunal had raised for Jasper Infotech—then a couponing business, had been exhausted. Salaries to the tune of Rs 5 lakh had to be paid to the company's 15 odd employees the very next day. This meant, the only option remaining was to empty out their personal bank accounts, and subsist on a princely sum of Rs 30,000 (the balance remaining after dues were cleared), till the end of the following month, when in all likelihood employees would have to be told that there was no money any longer to pay them!

Most in Rohit's situation would've buckled under and

taken the easy route out, assimilating into the multitudes that go to office each day and return with a pay cheque that denotes surety and security for so many of us in life. After all he was a computer engineer from IIT with great prospects in the job market.

But like a fierce, fearless, true-blooded entrepreneur with a vision to fulfil, Rohit chose the difficult alternative. He shook out of the comfort zone his mind was subconsciously veering him towards, donned his risk-taker hat and decided to walk the road less travelled. And soon enough, as if magically, the barriers fell away, the fears disappeared and opportunities he couldn't have dreamt of from a long shot presented themselves one after another.

It wasn't divine intervention. To stand unwavering, remain mentally focused, discover one's true calling and put in your whole and soul into actualizing a dream at a time when all odds are stacked up against you needs strength of character not many possess. Rohit is among the few that did, and for entrepreneurs that in itself is half the battle won. Success then hinges on several other variables—luck, timing, access to capital, ability to implement—all of which in his case collided to make it happen.

But for a majority of entrepreneurs crossing that first barrier of perseverance is in itself a test they seldom pass.

BOY FROM MALOUT

Rohit Bansal was born in Malout (pronounced Maa'lot).

You would be wan trying to locate it on a map, had it not been for the internet. But it is a relatively prominent town today, occupying an interesting site along the NH-10 Grand Trunk Road in Punjab's cotton belt. Malout shares a border with three states—Punjab, Haryana, and Rajastan, and two countries—India and Pakistan (which is barely 40 kms away). Bhatinda, made famous, courtesy Jab We Met, the popular 2007 Bollywood flick, is the largest city in its vicinity.

'It was the kind of town in which streets would be lined up with cots in the summer. Where entire families could be seen sleeping under the sky when there was a power cut,' describes Rohit. 'Even Meerut, which would otherwise not be considered amongst the largest cities of India, felt like a big city to us.'

This is precisely why it is difficult to imagine that Rohit the urbane, erudite co-founder of India's largest online marketplace, doyen of a futuristic technology enabled business, grew up in this dusty agrarian outpost. He is the very antithesis to the kind of person one would imagine an ordinary boy from Malout would be. And Snapdeal, provides such a glaring contrast to the businesses his father, grandfather, and their forefathers built over generations, that one is left scrambling to spot traces of the awkward, rural boy who could barely cobble up a sentence in English by the time he had passed his tenth standard.

Jagannath Bansal, Rohit's grandfather had migrated to Malout from an even smaller village called Rama to start a small grain merchandise dealing. He was an influential figure at the municipal level and had made quite a name for himself by the time he handed over the reins to his two sons Ramesh Kumar and Vijay—Rohit's father and uncle. Ramesh had got himself a bachelor's degree in pharmaceutical sciences from the Panjab University at Chandigarh but couldn't digest the idea of working for someone else and so left his job on the third day to join the family business, which he ran jointly with his brother.

'They basically procured grain from farmers and sold to government granaries like the Food Corporation of India or the APMC markets, eventually getting a fertilizer distributorship, which was a natural progression in the trade,' explains Rohit.

The family's fortunes hinged a great deal on the vagaries of nature. It was an environment in which no two days were the same. 'Our fate changed with seasons, with the weather playing truant, with alien weed species producing problems,' says Bansal, which explains partially his belief that it is an inherent comfort with uncertainty—a characteristic incubated by a childhood in which the family's cash position would dramatically vary from day to day—that made him a good entrepreneur.

When Rohit was in class six, ground water levels in the area rose up, inundating most of the land. Crops failed for several years, as cotton in particular is susceptible to unseasonal rains. There was nothing to sell and no recovery from farmers. It was a tough time and Ramesh, who would otherwise sit by the window watching the rain slide down, was despondent that his fortunes had been washed away.

'It was a strange feeling to be at the mercy of nature,' says Rohit. 'All one could do was wait. If nothing else, it taught me patience, a quality entrepreneurs need in abundance.'

Alongside patience, if one possessed above average intelligence, it was a winning combination. And as a boy at Sacred Heart Convent School, the only English medium school in town, Rohit was a brilliant student. He topped class and possessed a raw intelligence that made school education a cinch.

'I met him only in class 11, but it was evident very quickly that Rohit was the class brain,' says Kunal. 'From mathematics to computers, what took others two pages to solve a problem, would take him three lines.'

As he continued doing well in school, the reality that he wouldn't join his family business became clearer. His parents were okay with that. They were quite unlike other folk in town and never let him take for granted the fact that he had a family undertaking to fall back on. That, they rightly felt would be taken as a way out of bad performance in academics and they didn't want Rohit to have a false sense of entitlement.

This attitude left the boy with time to mull over endless career choices. Business always excited him and he'd often accompany his father to their shop, fascinated by the lively buzz of the place where his dad interacted with customers and conducted day to day transactions. But in a small town with no internet or satellite TV, ambitions were shaped by what one saw or heard around them, or what elders in the family considered as 'good' professions for a topper student. Someone suggested IAS, so for the longest time without knowing what it entailed, Rohit nurtured ambitions of getting into the civil services. Others reckoned the IITs were the places to go to.

What was written in stone, however, was that if you got above 90 percent in class 10 and cleared the NTSE (National Talent Search Examination) you would head to Delhi Public School. Rohit had made the cut on both counts.

SMALL FISH IN BIG POND

1999—the year he cleared his boards was the only one in which two students from Malout were selected to go to Delhi Public School. Puneet and Rohit, the two toppers from their division, confident young teens, who had till date marched through school education with a chip on their shoulders, headed for Delhi. They would find themselves with sweaty palms as they sat for the lecture on day one.

'I'd formally been educated in an English medium school, but didn't quite know how to speak the language. So, when the class teacher began asking for introductions in English, I panicked,' laughs Rohit. He remembers by-hearting his introduction as he waited his turn.

Delhi was a major change of scene. After being treated like a classroom hero back in Malout, he had now to contend with several other intelligent, more confident peers. And a lack of fluency with the English language even gave him a slight inferiority complex. For months, the boy spoke only in monosyllables.

While academically he managed to stay right at the top, the change in milieu took time to get accustomed to. Rohit had till then had it very easy, never having to struggle or work hard at achieving good grades. But for the first time, he felt like the proverbial small fish swimming in a big pond. He could have been overwhelmed by it all, had it not been for a new friend he made barely a month into the term.

Enter Kunal Bahl—the diametric opposite—a city boy, self-assured, and very articulate. 'Our initial friendship was based very much on food and dirty jokes,' quips Rohit, but it really began when the two found a common *bakra* whose leg they could pull on the back benches.

'The not-to-be-named guy was a fairly unexceptional character, who'd nevertheless boast about this that and the other,' he remembers. 'We'd invariably sandwich him between the two of us and give him a piece of our mind. It was a friendship that began with our collective aversion to pretentious people.'

And it grew. The two sat together on the same bench till they passed out of junior college and as Rohit calls it, formed a closed knit group that consisted of just the two of them. No other friends. Both shared a passion for food and Rohit being stuck with inedible hostel fare would be fed by Kunal's mother, who packed extra lunch for him in the tiffin. On weekends he'd be invited over to have home cooked meals.

'I was vegetarian till then. No one in my extended family,

let alone at home had eaten meat ever. But Kunal converted me.' When not in class, the two would loaf the streets of Delhi in search of good food. Their usual hang outs were Chopsticks in South Delhi (because it had an unlimited Chinese lunch) and Nirula's at Priya Cinema—famous for its pizzas and sundaes.

'We'd have precisely Rs 130 needed for two hot chocolate fudges and the bus ticket to and fro,' remembers Rohit. Whoever knew back then that at Nirula's, over hot chocolate fudge, seeds were being sown for a great entrepreneurial partnership!

KUNAL BAHL - PARTNER IN CRIME

It was alas one such conversation, albeit several years later, over food (coffee to be precise!) that would trigger the idea that is today Snapdeal.com.

Rohit's story would be incomplete if told without Kunal's major presence and influence in his life, both professionally and on a personal level. They've known one another for more than half their lives and Rohit considers him a mentor-cum-friend. Kunal says Rohit is the third son his parents never had.

'In college he was always the droopy eyed, unhurried, chilled out character who'd fall asleep amid heated political discussions, while I was of the ambitious type-A disposition,' says Bahl, when quizzed about how different they are from one another and how their relationship has evolved over time.

Today Kunal has become milder while Rohit has gotten

more aggressive, even if in his own silent determined manner. And it is these complimentary differences between the two that several observers reckon, are responsible for the great success they've seen professionally. As clichéd as it might sound, Kunal and Rohit complete one another. The former is the media savvy face of Snapdeal, a marketing wizard who looks at softer functions like HR, investor relations and branding, while Rohit is the quiet data-driven, analytical brain, who focuses on technology, logistics, and other technical functions.

'I am the CEO and he is the COO, but that is just a matter of the roles we play. For all practical purposes both of us run the company as co-chairmen, looking after different tasks,' says Kunal, in all earnestness.

It was a natural gravitation towards their roles and quite unplanned, explain the duo, who, despite the clear segregation in their functions constantly roll up into each other to bounce off ideas and 'prick one another's bubble' so that neither gets carried away in the wrong direction.

As they've become more successful over the years there has set in a comforting equilibrium in their equation. Kunal narrates how in the early days, in the absence of anything else they'd disagree on every little point—from the colour of a logo to the size of the font. Today however, no matter what ideological differences they may have about a certain issue, they make it a point not to let the world know.

'We get into a room, thrash out our differences and ensure that when we walk out only one point of view is disseminated to the rest of the team,' Bahl explains, giving an insight into how the top management at Snapdeal is encouraged to function.

If the rapport at work is enviable, outside office it is stronger. The simple rule of thumb is that they either do things together or don't do it at all. Which is why their financial portfolios look alike, their investments are identical and outside the ambit of Snapdeal they share similar passions. One of which is nurturing new entrepreneurs who solicit their help.

Even as they grow the company, they have in their personal capacities jointly seed funded several early stage companies as angel investors—Ola Cabs, Unicommerce, Housing.com, and Agro Star to name the prominent ones—and insist that their strength multiplies when they lean on one another for support. 'We know individually our decision making is incomplete and weak,' admits Kunal.

Both credit the years they spent building Snapdeal together—the triumphs, the tribulations, the stumbling blocks along the way, the good and bad decisions, the remedial measures—as their real university.

The years preceding it—when Kunal headed out to U-Penn and Wharton, and Rohit to IIT—after DPS was just a long interlude. But for Rohit, quite an eventful one!

IIT - DELHI AND COMING OF AGE

In his fourth year at IIT Delhi, Rohit Bansal, the brilliant topper from Malout, flunked two courses in one semester.

What also happened incidentally was that he was almost thrown out.

One fine morning, two days before his results were due, Rohit walked into his course advisor's office in order to get his signatures for admission into the next semester.

'How did it go Rohit?' asked the distinguished professor, whom he'd rather not name. The man was a very senior faculty who everybody feared.

'Okay,' replied Rohit casually.

As it turned out, his results were not in fact 'okay'. And three days later he got a letter from his department, which said that a student review committee would be evaluating his case because he had failed in two courses. Students conceivably under stress or unable to perform because of some reason or the other would usually be appraised by such committees.

Rohit told them he would do extra courses in the next semester to be able to finish his graduation on time. To do this however, he needed the approval of his course advisor. When he went to get it, the man was fuming!

'Two days ago young man... you told me you'd done okay in your exams and now you have the audacity to ask me for permission to take additional courses despite failing two subjects?!' he hollered.

Rohit apologized, begged, pleaded and tried every other trick in the book, but he just wouldn't sign the document. Every morning for the next 60 days he would knock on the professor's door, but to no avail. What's worse, the IITs had no procedure to deal with a scenario wherein because a course advisor had refused to sign a document, a student couldn't take on additional work to finish his/her course on time.

'Even the dean was helpless when he figured who my advisor was, such was the stature of this man,' recalls Rohit.

Finally just in the nick of time, his Head of Department came to the rescue. The only option remaining was to change his advisor, who would finally approve Rohit's plea and let him move ahead to the next semester.

Instances like these and also his vacillating emotional state made IIT a bittersweet memory. Nevertheless the five years he spent there between 2001 and 2006 brought about profound changes in his personality. For one, he found himself in the company of several who were more distinguished than him and realized that excellence didn't necessarily begin and end with academic performance.

'I hadn't read a single book till I stepped into the IIT-D campus. Not even a Jeffrey Archer, the first of which I picked up whilst at campus. Suddenly I was in an environment where I was exposed to the concept of a life beyond marks and academics.'

But for a boy from Malout, to get into IIT was a very big deal indeed. With the exception of one gentleman, who had gotten in sometime in the 1980s, nobody had ever achieved such a feat and Rohit became somewhat of a local celebrity when news of his admission reached home. 'The myths, the legends surrounding the fabled IITs sent my town into a tizzy,' he laughs.

But, if the fact that he had clinched the seemingly

unattainable seat was seen as a once in a lifetime opportunity by many, Rohit took his IIT tag rather casually. This was partly a factor of the fact that for an IITian, a job, no matter how badly one fared in an examination, was guaranteed and it was still five years away. But more importantly existential dilemmas about what success meant, what the purpose of life was, and why one had devoted so much time and energy all along towards the seemingly banal idea of rote learning was beginning to throw him off balance. He continued to do brilliantly in courses he liked—algorithms, psychology, dramatics, and fared horribly in ones he didn't—networks, operating systems and the like (which is strange because he was a computer science student).

His vulnerability was to some degree exacerbated by his newly found penchant for dystopian European novelists. From Plato's Republic to Aldous Huxley's Brave New World, Kafka, Orwell, and Immanuel Kant to academic theories on evolution and texts on world philosophy, he soaked it all in. At one point reading became such an obsession that the moment he got off college he'd immerse himself into the world of the 'esoterics' to try and understand the complexities of the human condition.

It was no surprise then that his academic performance suffered, oscillating between 9.1, which was considered brilliant, to as low as 4.1.

A three-month internship at Waikato University in Hamilton, New Zealand, during his third year proved thankfully to be a turning point. As most of his cohorts on the four-year program were getting ready to graduate, Rohit who'd enrolled in the five year computer science degree program packed his bags and left for Hamilton. 'It was a fantastic experience. The three months there helped add a lot of depth to my personality,' he says.

For the first time in his life, he realized that there were people who spent time alone, that college didn't always have to be a collaborative exercise. That one could introspect in solitude and find answers to niggling questions. The much needed isolation from friends brought about a realization that he had pretty much wasted his years at IIT and needed to recoup from a routine of lassitude. It also dawned on him that if he were to do anything meaningful in life, it would have to be something he absolutely loved.

So back in Delhi three months later, with little more than a year before he would pass out of IIT, Rohit put in all his rigor on academics and scored a 9. Usually the penultimate semester is a time for students to slack because they get placed by the end of the first six months. But for Rohit the reverse held true. It was obligatory for him to clear all his courses on time in order to bag a job when the placements season would kick in.

Having begun working with exclusion, Rohit's theory was that he'd rather wait it out and sit jobless, than do something unexciting. That pretty much ruled out a software role in a large IT company, no matter that it was one of his core subjects and also a hot profession to get into at the time.

The most coveted companies came to campus in the first

three days of the placements season, but Rohit didn't bother with them at all. While visiting home in his semi-depressed state a few months earlier, his worried parents had even told him they had given up all hope of their son landing a decent job. For the very first time, his concerned dad also offered to have him join the family business. But Chinkle, his elder sister casually advised him to look for work in the US for a change of scene. That had caught his fancy.

And as luck would have it, the only company that placed students in the US—Capital One—a renowned Richmond headquartered financial services behemoth was coming to campus to recruit fresh graduates on the eleventh day. Analytics was also an area which was of relative interest to Rohit, so in what seems with hindsight like a bold, risky bet, he decided to apply only for this one role. And fortunately they offered him a place.

'I remember getting a call at 8 pm letting me know I was hired. I was ecstatic. As if with the flick of a switch I transformed from this clueless, unhappy guy unsure about my future, to somebody who had a mission to accomplish,' he remembers.

Life had a new purpose, so what followed were frantic months of studying to clear the course backlog. With a 9 in the last semester, Rohit graduated from IIT with an overall score of seven—not too bad for someone who had put in minimal effort.

The parents were overjoyed, and batch mates flummoxed. 'That guy?!...How?' was the universal reaction.

CAPITAL ONE

Destiny they say is not a matter of chance, but a matter of choice. In Rohit's case this didn't hold true. Barely weeks after joining Capital One, he would find out that he wasn't fated to go to the US after all. They had applied for his visa, but the limit for the H1B quota ran out and so he was asked to move to Bangalore instead, with a promise that he would be sent to the US a year later.

Alas, even that was not to be. This time not because the visa didn't come through, but because of his own doing. Kunal Bahl, his old friend, had by this time begun working for Microsoft after graduating from Wharton. The duo had kept in touch despite being 7000 miles apart and would meet when Kunal came down to India a couple of times every year. Rohit would even do his computer science assignments that Kunal found very hard to do. The two were still best buddies and would often bounce off ideas to one another over email on potential businesses they could start together some day.

'He was surer about entrepreneurship, I was a bit tentative, but Kunal talked me into it quite quickly,' says Rohit, who decided fairly out of the blue, a few months before he was due to leave for America, that US could wait, entrepreneurship was more exciting. 'It happened during Kunal's brother's wedding, when I flew down to Delhi to be with his family.'

A day after the functions were over and done with, Kunal gently broached the topic. Rohit casually nodded in agreement, but Kunal had made up his mind to act swiftly.

He was very serious and told Rohit to come home the very next day to brainstorm.

Neither had envisaged that they would lock themselves in a room for the whole of the next week in the course of which they not only discussed multiple ideas but also firmed up their decision to give up their thriving careers.

Wasn't it a HUGE risk?

'It was, but if I had to take it, that was the time. The IIT background and the work experience had instilled enough confidence in me to justify to myself that I could chart my own path, perhaps falter along the way, but never die hungry and poor,' he says. 'It was a two-five minute decision, and ever since most other major choices in my life—whether it is to do with marriage, adopting a particular business model, or a marketing campaign—have been two-five minute decisions.'

Convincing the bosses at Capital One was a difficult task though. A twenty three year old upstart giving up a dollar salary and a great job was considered madness. And Sarvottam, Rohit's immediate boss at Capital One did all he could to convince the young man that he was being unreasonable in quitting barely a few months into his first job ever. So much so that a meeting had to be set up with the MD of the company Atma Iyer in a bid to stop him from resigning. 'It was a tough conversation, but I told him even if I failed miserably, thirty years later I didn't want to leave room for regret that I hadn't tried.'

Eventually, once they were sure that Rohit wasn't merely being trigger happy, but had thought through his decision and was making an informed choice, they encouraged him to follow his instinct. But at home all hell broke loose. While the parents were happy that he wouldn't be going to the US, members of Rohit's extended family were convinced he didn't have his head in the right place any longer.

'The fact that I was giving up what was for many a dream, was considered sacrilege.' Rohit ignored their skepticism anyhow and by October 2008, barely a year into his stint at Capital One, moved to Delhi. Kunal too relocated after six years in the US, interestingly after being deported, and thus began their entrepreneurial journey in the latter's bedroom.

A FLEDGLING ENTERPRISE

In that fateful week when the duo had locked themselves inside Kunal's bedroom, they thought up a dozen ideas big and small. A portal for instance that reviewed products and services was discussed. They even registered a rather obscure sounding Spanish domain name called Miscalo. But Mouthshut.com was already in existence and so that was summarily canned.

Another one they actively pursued before it fizzled out, was a site that would rate the extant e-commerce players in the market. And there were many of those back then—eBay, Indiatimes, Indiaplaza and so on.

The brainstorming carried on even after the week came to an end and a couple of months into this active ideating period they froze on what seemed like a very doable business—online movie ticketing. Very quickly, a domain name Moviebookings.com was registered, and the duo began initial research about the size and scope of the market, spoke to multiplex companies, even discussed the look, color and feel of the site. But, just when it seemed like the venture was about to take off, Bookmyshow.com got funded by media giant, Network 18. Daunted by the event, this plan too was scrapped.

Having lived in the US as a student, the physical couponing services business had always intrigued Kunal. As a devout foodie with little money in his pocket he'd always be on the lookout for cheap restaurant deals and as a result would pick up the local offline entertainment publications for its coupons which offered sweet deals on meals. It was back then a $350 million business in the US and since India too was seeing a boom in direct marketing and offline retail, both Kunal and Rohit felt they could replicate the same story back home.

They spent four months doing what felt at that point intense research and ground work before launching their start-up. 'The two years from then on was when our real college began,' says Rohit. 'What we hadn't learnt in two decades, those 24 months of practical training taught us.'

From how a product is designed, marketed and sold to the legalities of incorporating a company to finance and HR management, the two were literally thrown into the deep sea. They had to very quickly figure out how to keep their heads above the water. It was baptism by fire, but also an interesting phase, because, while the coupon book business seemed like a brilliant idea at the outset, little did the duo know that making it work would be easier said than done.

Their first challenge was convincing potential employees to join their team. A month after starting the company in Kunal's bedroom, they moved the enterprise into a semi-legal make shift office in the basement of a residence at Kirti Nagar furniture market. It was a terrible place and most candidates would return half way simply because they couldn't find the address.

'Get into the furniture market, take a left after the police station and cross the big black gate. Once you do that, go around the broken Maruti car and ring the bell. The instructions were simple really,' laughs Rohit at the memory. 'Wonder why no one could find it!'

In India, founder entrepreneurs who called up candidates themselves for an interview weren't taken seriously. They needed to build an aura of importance around them. So the duo put Kunal's sister-in-law on the job. She was the 'HR head' and would direct people to office. Once the candidate got there, either of the two would go outside to greet the interviewee.

'If he/she was there to meet Kunal, I would fetch them and say Mr Kunal is tied up, so please sit for a few minutes. If someone had come to meet me, Kunal would greet the person and pretend I was busy. That was the only way we could prove that we meant business and weren't a bunch of clueless kids trying to set up a company.'

The initial days were tough though. Very tough. If convincing potential employees to join their team was hard, persuading others to buy their coupon was an even tougher task.

They toiled hard. With long excel sheets opened in front of them, they spent hours cold calling CEOs, pleading with potential merchants to partner them for discounts, waited outside offices with the hope of meeting a mid-rung manager who could help them clinch a deal.

'I once sat at a reception three days in a row to meet a manager,' remembers Rohit. 'He finally got fed up and met me.' At restaurants, the two would have a meal and then convince the owner to come on board as a merchant. Attitudes would change instantly as they metamorphosed from being customers to sellers of a business proposition.

'People shooed us away. But our code name for gate crashing an office was "standing ovation" and we gave several such ovations,' laughs Rohit.

The hard work gradually paid off and several established brands did agree to partner with them—from Dominos Pizza to Ferns & Petals, Reebok, Adidas, Levi's as well as several local restaurants and spas came on board. The first battle was won and a whole nine months later 'Money Saver'—a booklet laden with discounted coupons was brought to the market.

The launch was a colossal failure. Barely three people bought their booklet from across the four stalls they had set up to sell the coupons! This was a crisis because the duo had hugely overestimated demand and audaciously printed

50,000 booklets, using up a majority of the angel funding they had managed to garner from an angel investor in the US for printing.

The problem was, they were trying to achieve the impossible—a perfect invention. And in that pursuit endless amounts of time was spent debating the superfluities—the look, the color, the font, the precise placement of the UV fibre, so that the coupon wouldn't be forged. What the two didn't focus on were the fundamentals—how and where they were going to sell, how big their target market was, whether people would believe in the authenticity of a booklet that two nonentities were selling for Rs 399, what they needed to do to convince people that the discounts were real and not a hoax.

'Our dreams came crashing down. Because at least 10,000 people had walked past the stalls we'd put up and only three of them saw it fit to spend their money on the coupon booklet. Something had gone horribly wrong.'

A month passed by and barely a 100 coupons were sold. Customers were now even more unwilling to buy because a booklet with six months validity had perishable inventory and they had already lost a month. Thankfully, what salvaged the situation was that B2B customers found the business reliable and somehow the two convinced a few credit card companies to bundle the coupon booklet as a welcome gift for customers only just managing to recover the printing cost.

But that was just a temporary breather. Through several such trials and errors two years went by and the duo dabbled in numerous businesses—from mobile coupons to scratch cards—until that one dreadful day in 2009 when the time for experimentation was finally up. The company had reached a finish line on finances. Nothing seemed to be working out and this was when Rohit felt for the very first time after quitting Capital One that it was time to give up and get back to a 9-5 job.

Amid talks of folding up he also got married.

LUCK BY CHANCE

'Convincing Parul's parents proved to be a difficult task. Much harder than convincing investors, who were used to dealing with young and often audacious entrepreneurs. '"Couponing? What's that?" they asked me when I told them what I did for a living,' chuckles Rohit, recounting how his in-laws needed much wooing before they agreed to give their daughter away to him.

But marriage proved lucky for him. Parul brought with her a stroke of good fortune. Even though the company had reached a precipice financially, Money Saver as a brand was getting established among merchants, some of whom had begun prodding the duo to consider taking their business online—a proposal that provided the first trigger for launching Snapdeal.com.

Around the same time they also met Vani Kola, their first investor who agreed to bail them out just in the nick of time. The confluence of these two factors is what firmed up their conviction to start a deals portal.

MEETING VANI

Vani Kola—entrepreneur turned venture capitalist at IndoUS Ventures—put in money where her mouth was, when 23 other private equity firms had shown Rohit and Kunal the door. Like they would to CEOs, the duo had cold emailed her with the hope that she would one day call them for a meeting. Most others had rejected their business idea saying their model was not scalable or that their target market was very small, but Vani saw a spark and decided to give them a chance.

'I liked them instantly,' says Vani. 'We invest only in 2 percent of the companies that we meet because most entrepreneurs come unprepared and without as much as a clue that I am Ms and not Mr Vani Kola. These two had done their homework well.'

What she loved in particular was how thoughtful their email was. It laid out concisely the plans they had—to build an organization that was focused by data driven decision-making, that aspired to reach a large size by focusing on SMEs and 'something about bringing a new dimension to consumer engagement'. They hadn't yet specified it would be a website selling deal.

A meeting was arranged in Bangalore and within two days, IndoUS Ventures committed $2 million dollars. 'It was an unbelievable feeling,' recounts Rohit. 'The fact that a seasoned entrepreneur and investor was backing us was a bigger validation of our belief in what we were doing, than the thrill of getting a few million dollars.'

But his account of the meeting with Vani varies slightly from hers. If she thought it went very well, both Rohit and Kunal felt it had been a disaster. 'We were naïve and had presented six ideas—from loyalty cards to a direct mailing service called Easy Shopper to something on rebates to online coupons. She reprimanded us almost like a teacher saying "Guys...you are a ten people company, how will you do six different businesses?" Focus instead on one business that will attain critical mass.'

It was only Vani's way of telling them what seemed wrong with their approach, while trying to spot all along what was right with their thought process. But they felt she had told them off. '(Laughs) Perhaps they were taken in with the intensity of my questioning, but that is only a good sign. If I am not asking questions, I am not interested in you,' says Vani.

Rohit remembers harbouring a great degree of skepticism about going online initially. He didn't want to do anything to disrupt the status quo as couponing was just beginning to gather steam. All the same, it was for the first time that he and Kunal were beginning to notice a change. Earlier they were the ones pleading with merchants to partner them on Money Saver. Now the scenario had reversed and they were the ones being prodded to launch a deals portal so that the affiliation could carry on online. Both he and Kunal concluded it would be imprudent to ignore these calls. Also, jumping in before competition intensified in the segment was important.

SNAPDEAL.COM

It took hardly ten days from the time they sat at a Costa Coffee outlet to mull over the idea on the 26 January 2010, to the day the site was launched on 4 February 2010. Money Saver was rechristened Snapdeal—'Snap' representing speed and 'Deal' representing value. They spent $3000 for the URL which seemed like a princely sum at the time.

'We deliberated for an entire day on whether we should be spending this kind of mone,' remembers Rohit. Caution had set in because they had only just managed to rope in an investor while at the brink of closure.

The pre-launch days were exciting. Rohit hadn't taken a single day off in three years and the transition from offline to online made him busier than ever. His wife would be at sea about what was going on. He would come home late, rest for a couple of hours and then would be wide awake by 2 am furiously typing away an email to Kunal, who too would be burning the midnight oil. Neither slept very much as they worked with developers, designers and other technical staff to take the site live.

On 4 February, with a single deal—for a restaurant in Gurgaon called Salsa Salsa—Snapdeal.com went live. Parul, Kunal, and Rohit were the first customers and bought a coupon each (for a deal let you buy food worth Rs 500 for Rs 350). They also called every person they knew in Delhi and asked them to spread the word. By the end of the day they had sold five coupons which wasn't spectacular, but importantly, had begun receiving real feedback on which they acted swiftly.

'While offline we had spent months trying to build the perfect offering, this time our approach had changed diametrically. We decided to just dive in and tackle problems as and when they arose, and it worked,' explains Rohit. Core to this philosophy was paying close attention to insights and criticism gathered from merchants and consumers so as to tap the idiosyncrasies of the market and offer a service that was most relevant to local conditions.

A customer told them he was unsure about whether the company was legitimate. So promptly a landline number was put right at the top of the site. Another complained that he wasn't getting a confirmation voucher after making a payment, so they introduced that element too. A few months down the line buyers protested about the fact that they couldn't avail the offer of the day even if they wanted to because the location was too far out.

Unlike cities in the US, which were smaller and had one downtown area, Indian cities tended to be large and spread out, so replicating the American model of having just one deal per city wasn't working. It made sense to introduce a function whereby people could input their location and get a deal around their area. Such teething issues that one couldn't have predicted before consumers actually used the service came to the fore, and Snapdeal moved with speed to fix the loopholes.

This breakneck speed and ability to act on consumer feedback is what helped the company, considered by several in the industry as among the most nimble in India, grow into the behemoth it is today. Both Rohit and Kunal believe in an action-oriented approach, and do not like sitting over endless debates. Jump and make it happen has been their mantra which is reflected in the rapid evolution of Snapdeal from a company that sold discount coupons, to one that transitioned to online deals and now into India's largest broad focus e-commerce marketplace in just four years. They played around with the business model until they got it right

'They were agile, ready to listen and moved at the speed of light,' says Kola. 'They still do what it takes to keep the momentum. So, if that means for instance raising more capital to execute a particular plan, they will go ahead with it, and not get unnecessarily emotional about stake dilution, correct valuation and so on.'

No surprise it is that from being a site that offered one deal a day—for a local bar, restaurant, spa, or fitness class—two months into its existence, the site had begun offering hundreds of deals in multiple cities. Ten days after they went live in Delhi, Snapdeal launched in Mumbai. Within a couple of months ten more cities were added. From Pune and Chandigarh to Bangalore and Hyderabad, Kunal and Rohit would be on flights all month, recruiting people to set up offices. And in a matter of three months their employee force went up from 15 to 50 people. So staggering was the response that they gave up the offline coupons business entirely so as to concentrate on the site. The numbers initially were tiny—10 to 20 coupons a day—and the two would sit in office at the end of a hard day and wonder when they would sell 100 deals in a day.

It happened soon enough. In May 2010, they sold 100 coupons online on a Go-Karting deal. It was largely word of mouth publicity that was driving traffic, but this milestone told them that they were on to something really big.

And they were.

Just 14 months later, Snapdeal had garnered 70 percent of the market share. This was no mean feat. There were 30-40 players that had also begun operations around the same time—Taggle, Mydala, Dealsandyou—just to name a few. But many of them were pushed to the periphery because of the ruthless aggression the duo showed in expanding geographically.

'They were very future focused. They flourished because they invested in growth not for today but tomorrow,' says an observer.

One way in which they did this quite early on was by expanding inorganically. Snapdeal did its first acquisition five months into its launch. Whilst in Bangalore for a meeting, not one, but several merchants told Rohit that just like they loved working with Kunal and him, they also liked doing business with a company called Grabbon.

Almost immediately a meeting was set up with Sandeep Komaravelly and Tony Navin the co-founders and by July 2010 the two companies merged. 'We instantly connected because there were a lot of similarities in the way we thought, our values, and goals and vision for the future,' says Rohit.

'Grabbon was a small but high performance player and it made sense to collaborate and derive synergies.'

Post merger Tony began looking at the south market and Sandeep took over as marketing head. Both of them (Sandeep as SVP Marketing and Tony as SVP Electronics & Home) are today an integral part of the company and two among the ten people that make up the informal governing structure of Snapdeal. Since the Grabbon acquisition, Rohit and Kunal have gone on to buy several other smaller players with a view to either strategically expand their market in certain product categories or exploit technology platforms. Shopo, eSportsBuy (which it shutdown subsequently) and more recently Doozton.com, an online product discovery technology platform that enables the site to personalize how it lists and suggests fashion merchandise to users are among the few.

BUILDING THE MARKETPLACE

By mid-2011 both Rohit and Kunal had become young hotshots. They began getting noticed and would be regularly featured in magazines and newspapers. Snapdeal was being written about all the time as it anticipated a Rs 100 cr turnover by the end of the year. It had expanded presence in 50 cities and boasted of 8 million members and 1.5 to 2 million unique visits to the site every month. So rapid was the pace of growth that an office space leased out for three years in Okhla Industrial Estate with a capacity to accommodate 95 employees filled up in just 6 months.

Importantly, in that year the company also did another round of fundraising. A total of $40 million from two global investors—Bessemer Venture Partners and Nexus Venture Partners. 'Our goal was to induct entrepreneurial investors who could understand our pains and turmoil easily and wouldn't course correct us too much while we made our decisions,' says Rohit, who credits his investors for being brilliant sounding boards with whom the two forged a very open relationship. Such comfort with investors was necessary because in that year, Snapdeal would undergo dramatic changes.

Acting again upon the repeated requests of their customers and merchants Rohit and Kunal decided to take a leap of faith and transition from being a mere deals company to an e-commerce marketplace modeled on the Chinese giant Alibaba—a feat that wouldn't have been as smooth without the support and encouragement of those that were funding their start up. More so because things were going just great and there was no need for a disruption in the status quo.

'The motivation to shift from deals to products was a result again of listening carefully to consumer feedback. We began getting multiple requests from buyers and merchants asking why along with deals on spas, restaurants and gym programs, we didn't also offer deals on products like perfumes, pen drives or clothes as well,' says Rohit

These recurring requests puzzled the duo because several e-commerce players already existed in the market. But they decided to give it a shot anyway and sold their first product—a pair of Reebok sunglasses—as a pilot to test the market. The response was staggering. Within two days 4000 pieces were sold.

'Consumers were flocking our portal because they were transacting with us on coupons as it is and so trusted the site to also deliver to them a product of their choice. It was the reliability factor I think, along with the fact that other e-commerce companies of the time didn't have a very large selection that gave us an advantage,' explains Rohit, when quizzed about why consumer response was so good. Anyhow, products continued to remain an auxiliary business for the site which began with only one deal a day.

It was a trip to China however that year, which brought about a theatrical shift in how they approached their business. Every investor the duo had met was telling them to visit China. So after fixing up a few meetings with Chinese e-commerce companies, they bought tickets for a three-day whirlwind trip to Beijing and Shanghai. It proved to be a game changer.

'Indian e-commerce was at that point a 5000 products a day market all put together, but standing there in the middle of a fulfillment centre in Beijing and seeing 2.5 lakh orders get processed physically was a surreal experience. It blew us away completely,' remembers Rohit.

China gave him a glimpse into the potential e-commerce had back in India and firmed up his resolve about chasing the dream back home. A meeting with Hans Tung (who subsequently put in an undisclosed sum for a stake in Snapdeal) at his house in the outskirts of Beijing further consolidated that belief. Here was a man, who had put his money into the Chinese e-commerce boom, telling Rohit and Kunal how eerily similar to the India of 2011, the Chinese retail market place had been in the early 2000s.

Several companies had expanded into organized retail, opening all kinds of stores in the early part of the millennium. But as real estate prices shot through the roof and rents soared, growth got stunted and retailers couldn't expand further with margins getting squeezed out. (In China as in India, real estate costs constitute 7-8 percent of sales as compared to 0.5-1 percent for US retailers like Wal-Mart). Chinese consumers, meanwhile, were getting richer as the economy grew and internet penetration increased, creating demand for aspirational products that brick and mortar retail was unable to service. What filled this gap was e-commerce and the smartest and largest among them was a company named Alibaba, whose staggering success inspired Rohit and Kunal to replicate its mirror image back home.

Jack Ma promoted Alibaba today accounts for 80 percent of China's online retail transactions and sells $250 billion worth of merchandise, eclipsing the volumes on both eBay and Amazon combined according to onc estimate. It works on the marketplace model and holds zero inventory, unlike an Amazon, which is to say that it merely operates a technology platform to connect a scattered group of suppliers to buyers and acts as a liaison between the two.

E-commerce players across the world have used divergent models to grow but Alibaba gathered scale very quickly because it solely focused on solving the problem of access through its execution capabilities without actually holding any physical stock of the goods it sold. Snapdeal modeled itself around Alibaba and was the first player to imitate this asset light, capital efficient model when other companies in India like Flipkart (which in 2013 changed over to the hybrid inventory cum marketplace model) were expanding using the inventory-based model.

This, Rohit says, let them grow to roughly the same size as other players, but without the need to scramble for infinite space, planning, or money, unlike its rivals who've often been accused by critics of guzzling millions of dollars in what is seemingly a bottomless pit. It has also let Snapdeal remain a lean organization with a workforce of 1500 vis-à-vis 7000-8000 in other e-commerce set ups of a similar size.

'We realized early on that there was no point stocking inventory and treading the paths thousands of retail, logistics and courier companies had paved over decades. Which is why we decided to act as enablers and partner with rather than compete with them.' Marketplaces are however difficult to execute and pose complicated challenges, particularly in areas like order fulfillment and logistics management. They also must make do with lower margins compared to inventory led companies, even though volumes transacted are higher. Nonetheless the decision to make the shift to a marketplace was true to tradition a two-five minute one.

'We came back from our meeting with Hans and were sitting at a Starbucks outlet in Beijing. I was bubbling with excitement, but waiting for Kunal to confirm that he shared my enthusiasm too,' remembers Rohit. 'Thankfully both of us felt the same level of conviction separately.'

Back in India, on a late Friday evening, Rohit immediately summoned the head of product management for a meeting outside office the next day. The site had a UI (user interface) revamp planned for Monday, which was delayed by a week. The design had several columns for deals and barely a line at the bottom for products. That was instantly turned around and products were placed right at the top.

On the following Monday, both Rohit and Kunal huddled with their teams and broke the news. It was easy to convince the team. What was more difficult was to get their investors to reconcile to the idea. Aside of the fact that the existing model was yielding results, investors were worried that changing over to a completely new business came with several associated execution risks. Inherent doubts that creep in when one isn't following the herd also led them to question whether the duo could pull it off. After all, why was no other e-commerce company in India building a marketplace back then?

It was only after much persuasion, that investors came on board. And what a wise move it was! Snapdeal would've been a careworn peripheral player struggling for survival, or perhaps even shuttered shop like several others had they decided against it.

THE TRANSITION

The transition was daunting remembers Rohit and 2012 was a year of high decibel activity. 'It was like starting from scratch and rebuilding a new company altogether. From logistics to category management, technology to customer service, all the elements in this business were vastly different from those in a deals company, and no one in our team knew anything about how a broad focused marketplace functioned.'

Very quickly the duo moved their smartest people to take charge of the new venture. They didn't pause to breathe and improvised along the way. Everything needed an overhaul—from technology for tracking-delivery-payment to category management to the search functionality to the approach of customer care, which needed to be reoriented from services to products. The pace was hectic. It took roughly a year for the switch and by the end of 2012, over 90 percent of Snapdeal's business came from products as opposed to 5 percent at the beginning of the year.

At the core of this success was the belief that what mattered solely was constructing a platform that hosted the largest assortment of new products in order to solve a consumer's problem of access. The zero-inventory business model enabled Snapdeal access to infinite shelf space and allowed an increase in assortment rapidly without deployment of too much capital into inventory, unlike its rivals. So much so that today a new product is added to the site every few seconds.

Fierce dedication to innovation on all operational fronts further helped the company power ahead swiftly in the next couple of years. It launched Safeship—a fulfillment technology platform with 100 percent traceability for buyers and sellers. Safeship integrated all courier companies in the country and in real time allocated orders depending on origin, source, type of product, past performance etc. This was done nowhere else in the world.

TrustPay—a fraud prevention mechanism modeled on Alibaba's AliPay was put to use to solve the problem of trust, which was a key deterrent to internet shoppers. It guaranteed purchases on Snapdeal by putting a customer's money into an escrow account for seven days and promising to return it should there be an issue with the product.

From their content management systems to fulfillment centres, quick innovation was used at every level to face up to the challenges that rapid growth posed. One company that was keeping a vigil on this brisk evolution was the global e-commerce giant eBay.

Rohit and Kunal had been in touch with them for about a year, having met several senior executives from the iconic San Jose headquartered company, merely to gain knowledge. They had no inkling that eBay's corporate development was closely watching their growth trajectory and would one fine morning send an email to the duo soliciting a meeting.

'One thing led to another and they said, why don't we invest. We were exhilarated because we needed capital and to have as knowledgeable an investor as eBay wanting to partner us just around that time was cherry on the cake.' 2013, thus began with a bang, as eBay invested in Snapdeal. Even though the first series amount remained undisclosed, a year later in early 2014, they increased their stake, putting in an additional $134 million.

'It is a hugely rewarding relationship,' says Rohit about the eBay partnership. Aside of the financial investment, operationally, eBay remains a source of infinite knowledge and experience for Snapdeal today. Whenever the company is in need of advice, eBay helps it reach out to their divisional experts to bounce off ideas. Meanwhile, Snapdeal has been teaching the global giant a thing or two as well.

'eBay found the work we did on our supply chain very interesting and is also looking at optimizing the Safeship function which we developed to bring a consistent delivery experience,' smiles Rohit, evidently proud.

The last two years have been remarkable for him and the company. On a very small base, the portal grew monthly sales six times in 2012. In 2013, on a much larger base with e-Bay on board, it expanded another six times and is today on its way to becoming a billion dollar company in revenue terms. According to *Forbes* magazine, Snapdeal has been growing at an astounding 500 percent annually compared to the industry average of 80 percent.

Meanwhile, investments into the company have been pouring in. Not only have global PE giants made a beeline, but some of India's most respected corporate tycoons too have put their money where their mouth is. In early 2014, along with e-Bay's second tranche, Snapdeal also raised $100 million from a group of five investors including Azim Premji's family office. And later in the year the legendary Ratan Tata put in an undisclosed sum into the company in his personal capacity, further validating the conviction others had already shown about Snapdeal's future prospects.

Rohit, is today one among the five trailblazer Bansals including Sachin and Binny of Flipkart, Mukesh of Myntra, and Peyush of Lenskart, who've come to dominate the Rs 12000-Rs 15000 cr e-commerce market in India in less than half a decade, each one defying their unique challenges to emerge winners.

Is there anything common among the Bansals that's eventually led them up this climb to success? They've dominated offline retail for centuries and this is perhaps an expected natural switch to the online sphere feels Kunal, the lone Bahl in this space.

And what a revolutionary switch it has been!

EVER EVOLVING

'I feel blessed to be a part of this story,' says Rohit, who looks at his journey as a once in a lifetime opportunity. He compares e-commerce today to what IT services was 15 years ago, or telecom was in the mid 2000s and says the next ten years will be India's e-commerce decade, a chance for large global companies to be built. Like telecom went from being 'nice to have' to 'need to have', e-commerce too will traverse that leg with internet penetration growing and India on its way to becoming the next global superpower.

But competition is getting ever more intense. Amazon with its global know-how and deep pockets has made its entry into India as a marketplace and Flipkart, Snapdeal's staunchest bigger rival has consolidated its presence by acquiring Myntra—India's largest fashion retailer. The former has just recently committed billions of dollars to ramp up its presence in the country, while the latter has been aggressively building a war chest from investors sending its valuations skyrocketing. All of these are signs of the faith investors have put into India's e-commerce future, but remaining relevant in this hyper-competitive environment is getting trickier by the day. From speed of delivery to discounts, product range to geographical reach, supply chain operations to technology platforms, the last year has seen companies engage in spirited games of one-upmanship in order to retain customers and prepare for future growth.

How then does Snapdeal plan to up its game?

'It will be a battle of philosophies rather than a battle of market share,' asserts Rohit, unperturbed, seemingly by the headway competition is making. The daily headlines on how much money rivals have raised don't bother him or Kunal. The latter has gone on record to state that Snapdeal is being aggressively pursued by internal and external investors wanting to pump in more capital whenever needed, but it is really a game of execution hereon rather than who raises most money. 'We are missionary in our pursuit to enable others to do e-commerce and not do it ourselves. By which I mean, we are committed, staying true to our marketplace business model,' says Rohit. 'And this model isn't very capital intensive.'

Amazon and others, he believes, are at heart inventory led companies even though they aren't positioning themselves any longer as being so in India. And Rohit's staunch conviction is that it is the marketplace which is most conducive for e-commerce to blossom in India. Globally large e-commerce businesses that have turned profitable are marketplaces like Alibaba and Taobao and not inventory led companies like Amazon, which has for long been burning cash, worrying analysts that it is stretching itself too thin with expensive investments.

He also takes comfort in the fact that Snapdeal has a lead over competition (and by a very high margin) on both the number of sellers on their platform and the number of categories in which they vend products. Their ever-increasing focus on mobile, 'when every other company is focused on building last mile delivery networks' also gives them a significant headway he believes. Over 50 percent of Snapdeal's consumers are mobile users and they are more loyal than those who buy on the PC.

Long-term focus on small vendors and non-metro consumers will also hold the company in good stead believes Rohit. Like Alibaba, which has over 50 percent of its sellers coming from tier-3 and tier-4 cities, Snapdeal also has a third of its vendors outside Metros and nearly two-thirds of its customers in tier-2 and below cities. 'The urban elite is a small sliver of the market. If e-commerce has to grow to the next stage, it needs to become relevant for everyone. It needs to participate in people's daily lives, where they start making core purchases online, not merely fancy bazooka items. Which is why our language is very different, our branding is more inclusive than our competitors,' he insists.

His Malout background comes of good use while penetrating the rural markets believes Kunal. Many small town insights that may not be obvious to others are noticeable to him. 'For instance, he is able to tell us, when we obsess over fast delivery that what matters to someone in a small town more is the availability of a large variety of goods at the best price, and not necessarily the speed.' Snapdeal today sells everything from soaps and moisturizers to home gyms, treadmills, children's swings and solitaire diamonds. And what comes up again and again is the assertion that they host the largest assortment of goods.

The company has also now entered newer territory. It launched an online education and digital learning marketplace in 2013, enabling consumers wanting to buy online education courses find a common meeting ground with content creation companies seeking to sell them.

The plan going ahead is to expand footprint into the digital services gamut generally. Travel and hotels? 'Perhaps,' says Rohit, not revealing too many details of what he has in mind. What he does assert, however, is that the next significant goal will be to turn profitable at a company level in the next two years in order to change the perception that online retailers have been indefinitely pushing that milestone in their pursuit for aggressive growth.

Rohit accuses critics fretting about profits as being myopic. They cannot visualize the scale e-commerce will reach tomorrow, he complains. 'You need to build a future for tomorrow, not for the present,' he says. 'Could these people have envisaged two years ago, when we were doing 2,000 orders a day that in early 2014 we will be shipping over 100,000 orders?'

Investors like Vani agree. The skepticism, she insists, stems from unfamiliarity with the sector and general lack of cultural support for what she sees as a bold, but carefully calculated strategy. 'You need stomach to compromise profit for growth. I have no doubt that within the next two years Snapdeal will make profits on a per order basis. Until then, with the base growing, it would be unwise not to make requisite investments in infrastructure, technology etc,' she adds.

In the same timeframe, Snapdeal will also go public in all likelihood, although the finer deliberations on this matter are yet to take place. There are plenty of ifs and buts, many more challenges and stumbling blocks along the way, insist skeptics. Constant comparisons with bigger rivals Flipkart and Amazon make newspaper headlines everyday and as Snapdeal paints the ever broadening e-commerce canvas, all eyes are on who will finally stake claim to becoming the next Alibaba of India.

The jury is still out, but there is no dearth of those that believe Snapdeal, despite being overshadowed today by the might of its competitors stands a very real chance. The market in India is big enough for a mix of large inventory led and marketplace driven companies to co-exist. In the vast e-commerce opportunity, the men have already been separated from the boys, and it will now be a market dominated by three-four big players. The challenge now will be how these companies differentiate so as to absorb a larger share of the incremental demand that will kick in, while simultaneously moving away from their discount association, which in the long run will prove to be unsustainable.

It is going to be an exciting race, one that will potentially change India, just the way mobile telephony, the railways or the IT services boom did, and one that Rohit says Snapdeal is geared to lead.

ON A LONG TRAIL

He has achieved at 31 what many don't in a lifetime. But one thing Rohit doesn't let happen, is allow the feeling of accomplishment get the better of him. Every day is still a struggle, if not to better the lofty benchmarks he's set for himself, or the soaring expectations other have from him, then to continually reinvigorate and inspire his team. Both he and Kunal pride themselves at driving a very entrepreneurial culture at Snapdeal, which is in a sense reflected in the quirky office space that the company occupies in Okhla Industrial Estate. Scarlet red paint, a welcome wall engraved with mottos, and cubicles buzzing with the vivacity of young whiz kids all of whom look to be between 25 and 30 years old.

'I am of the belief that as a company you need to be a bit *hatke* on the inside, to spread the same magic outside. We are a very high ownership organization—we encourage our employees to discuss goals with seniors, but execute the 'how' part with absolute freedom,' he says, giving an example of how a product manager had just a few months earlier come up with a proposal to construct a search on SMS functionality, and built the service in one month flat.

'Vision matters, but real innovation doesn't come from the top,' says Rohit. 'Because, only those closest to the customer know their pain points.' The mission is to nurture a bottom-up organization, and it is showing results. Several of Snapdeal's employees from the garage days are still with them and the composition of the senior management hasn't changed at all.

'He is very approachable. I can walk in and out of his or Kunal's cabin, not having to worry about the pecking order,' says an employee. Another calls him a 'quiet hero', someone who shuns grandiose and lets his work speak for itself. 'He is a great listener, you can debate with him and have a different point of view and he won't tick you off, which makes him a good leader.'

Kola, who's seen Rohit grow, agrees that all these qualities in him have only sharpened with time. 'I find the quiet confidence he exudes, the fact that he isn't larger than life and the high integrity he brings to the table charming in a world where the gregarious types are always pushing ahead,' she says. 'And with Kunal—that archetypal communicator with a brilliant knack to amplify the brand in tow, they've found a great rhythm.'

Both take pride in the fact that theirs is a compassionate business, one that has nurtured and empowered thousands of small entrepreneurs by giving them access to demand that was otherwise unreachable. One hears story after story in their office of a Kurti manufacturer for instance who'd once cycle from shop to shop in Karol Bagh convincing buyers to stock his clothes now selling thousands of pieces online. Or a middle-aged couple who've seen sales at their footware brand shoot up ten times as people from remote corners of the country reach out to them for orders. 'We want to create wealth and success for everybody. That is our core philosophy,' Rohit says earnestly.

But what does wealth mean to him personally? Success sometimes can corrupt, and if it is as meteoric as the sort he has seen in a span as short, it can overwhelm. Not this 31 year old though. 'I still drive the same car, travel economy, live in budget hotels and my hobbies—running, swimming, and adventure sports—barely require a good pair of shoes and a few thousand rupees every month for training. Yes, I no longer need to think twice before having an expensive meal with Kunal, so money is a source of comfort. Beyond that I don't think about it much.'

The joy of building a great company evidently far exceeds that of raking in the moolah. There is just that flash of insecurity sometimes, that all this success could evaporate someday and he'll fade into oblivion. But the mantra to steering clear of such ideas is to live for the day. 'I do have sleepless nights, not over whether we will be around 30 years from now though, but over how a particular problem in a fulfillment centre on a particular day will be resolved,' he laughs. 'I couldn't have imagined my present ten years ago, why bother then about my future ten years from now.'

Which is also why neither he, nor Kunal, has set a numeric vision for Snapdeal, even as rivals tom-tom about the size they are confident of reaching. There is quiet confidence though that even as the size of the e-commerce base grows, the endeavour will remain not only to retain a third of the market the company already has, but capture an even larger chunk of the pie.

With a task like that at hand, the credits must roll 'to be continued' rather than 'the end'...

MISSION SANITATION AND THE MAN BEHIND

R.K. Somany – HSIL

Every Sunday morning, in the 1950s, a young R.K Somany would drive to Behala, a neighborhood in the south-western fringe of Kolkata. His family owned a massive shooting range in the vicinity. Behala was then a relatively uninhabited periphery of the city, still to see the dawn of urbanization. RK would take along with him cartridges and his .22 rifle and blow up a minimum of 500 bullets at a time in target practice. He soon became a pro at shooting.

Over 50 years later, at the age of 77, he still retains that passion. RK has three licensed weapons—one gun, a revolver (weighing half a pound), and a pistol—all of renowned names. In addition, he also owns an air pistol. 'Put a matchstick in the garden and I can blow it up with my air pistol from ten feet away even today,' he tells me with a twinkle in his eyes.

He is self-trained in the art, just like he is in business. And shooting is a passion that has taught him the virtue of focus—a quality that helps him in his occupation and one that he laments is diminishing in today's youth.

There aren't many in the sanitary ware business in India who will not have heard of RK aka Rajendra Somany. He is an icon, a veteran in his sector, who commands respect and deference in equal measure. His company HSIL Limited, whose brand 'Hindware' is a household name today, brought into India the pioneering Vitreous China technology in collaboration with UK's Twyfords in the early 1960s.

But RK's career started off in the arms business—a sector far removed from the world of water closet, faucet, urinal, and wash basin manufacturing. He was, true to his calling for shooting, a civilian arms retailer.

In 1955, at barely 20 years of age, RK was literally pulled out of college and inducted into one of the many businesses his family owned. The company he was asked to look after was R.B. Rodda, the renowned London based retailer of civilian armory, firearms, guns, cartridges, and other outdoor gear that his brother had purchased from its British owners, who were getting ready to leave the country after partition. This is where his passion for shooting germinated and honed as the Behala range had come in as a package deal with Rodda's retail outlets when the company was bought over.

Rodda was among the five-six major arms retailers in India, alongside Lyon & Lyon, P. Orr and Sons, Walter Locke, and Manton. The brand originally established as Brown and

Rodda had offices in the UK and Calcutta between 1846 to 1955, when RK's eldest brother Hiralal Somany acquired it. Under RK's stewardship, Rodda & Co. would go on to become one of the largest importers of arms and ammunition.

'We shipped in the best of weapons for sportspersons from across the world and were the first ones to also begin installing telescopes on rifles,' RK boasts. All the products marketed were manufactured by top manufacturers globally and Rodda & Co. held a virtual monopoly in India.

But six years after he took over the reins, RK was ordered by his brother to pack his bags and head to the UK. Rodda was subsequently managed by Lalit Kumar, the youngest of the Somany siblings and eventually shutdown in the years to come as the business focus changed to manufacturing. 'The arms business became too "ticklish" to run,' he says.

It's two original showrooms still survive, but have been converted into sanitary ware outlets, the trade RK was destined to come into, far away from the seemingly exciting orb of arms and ammunition retailing.

GROWING UP

Somany is a great raconteur and has a vivid memory of his charming childhood in (then) Calcutta. He was born there in 1937, a year after his family made their humble beginnings as stockbrokers in the city. Growing up as the second youngest child in a large family of six brothers and three sisters, RK had a sheltered life with doting parents and siblings. His father

Murlidhar Somany died relatively early, when RK was barely seven and it was Hiralal his eldest brother and his wife, RK's affectionate *bhabhi*, who became his de facto parents.

'I owe all my initial success to him,' says RK about Hiralal, who had to assume the role of the family patriarch post Murlidhar's sudden death. Murlidhar was the adopted son of Ramprasad Somany, RK's paternal grandfather. Ramprasad came from a very well to do moneylender clan in Chirawa, a small village in the Jhunjhunu district of Rajasthan, known for its stunningly latticed Havelis. Like several of his contemporaries, the lure of the East, and the riches that a flourishing colonial trade promised brought him to Calcutta around 1905.

He undertook an arduous journey with his adopted son that lasted several days. The railways had not yet reached Chirawa and so it was on camel back that the father and son duo travelled all the way up to Kanpur, a distance of 530 kilometers. They would move through the day and pitch their tents at dusk for the fear of being looted of their meagre possessions. Bandits were always on the prowl they were told. Once in Kanpur, they left the camel behind and boarded the train to get to Calcutta.

The early days were tough. Ramprasad set up a trading business dealing in jute and gunny bags. His brothers and other extended family also migrated one by one and the Somanys made Calcutta their permanent base. By the 1930s, Murlidhar began dabbling in the stock markets as well and set up a broking business in which he made a fair amount of money. He had a tremendous zest for life and was very fond of racing. But a heart problem combined with an unholy cocktail of high sugar, high blood pressure, and hyper tension would be his undoing and he passed away a tad too soon.

It was barely a year after Murlidhar's death, in 1944, that the Somanys would set their foot for the first time in manufacturing. Several British owned companies and their sick plants were up for sale as colonial rule was gradually coming to an end. Hiralal saw an opportunity in the changing socio-economic environment and set up a small glass container manufacturing unit roughly 35 kilometres away from Calcutta. However, due to intermittent labour problem it had to be shut down.

Thereafter, in its place a semi-automatic glass manufacturing unit was put up at the Rishra premises a few years later. That is how Hindustan National Glass & Industries Ltd (HNGIL), today the country's largest manufacturer of container glass was born.

The Rishra unit continues to remain a major producer of glass bottles and is run by Chandra Kumar Somany and his family, RK's elder brother, who inherited the glass division post the family's split 20 years ago. It is now one of RK's key competitors as his own company HSIL (Hindustan Sanitaryware and Industries Ltd) has a large presence in the container glass manufacturing segment. Back then though HNGIL was a fledgling unit that marked the beginnings of the Somanys in manufacturing.

The family resided initially at Ratu Sarkar Lane near Calcutta's Central Avenue. Childhood was a time full of adventure and excitement for the young RK even as Hiralal was taking big strides in seeking new business opportunities. Dinner would characteristically be a noisy affair with everyone talking over one another. It was a large joint family set up typical of the Calcutta Marwaris of those days. The family resided in one of three similar bungalows on the lane.

The first of them was occupied by a certain Chajuram Chaudhury, a businessman who in those days had a dividend income of Rs 1 crore and drove a Rolls Royce. He was given the honorary title of Sir, given his stature in society and was always a source of fascination for the young RK.

Mahadev Somany RK's grand uncle and his family lived in the second bungalow, while the third house belonged to Murlidhar. It was the last house on the lane and marked an implicit boundary between the Hindus and Muslims residing in the city. In 1946, during the partition riots, the family found themselves in the midst of civil unrest and ultimately moved out of the house in Ratu Lane. A move which was triggered due to an unfortunate misunderstanding, which saw the family embroiled with the police.

Homes were often ransacked because of the infighting and so nights would be spent keeping a vigil on the terrace. Hiralal, his wife and RK would take turns every night and keep a watch. It was a traumatic time for the family and over the next few years they moved from one rented home to another and finally settled down in a house Hiralal built on Ironside

Road next to Ballygunge Post Office, close to the famous Birla Mandir which was not yet constructed then.

The violence and carnage still remains a vivid memory, says RK. It was amidst such hullaballoo that Somany finished schooling from the renowned St Xavier's Collegiate School for Boys, where he was taught by the same father Joris, who was Radheshyam Agarwal's principal. RK was enrolled in Xavier's in class one and left only after completing his class XII in 1958, so much of his formative influences were drawn from life in school and college, which he had to fight to complete.

After class twelve, Onkarmal, RK's second eldest brother told him to join the family business as an extra pair of hand to support the day to day working at office. RK was shattered as further studies were on his mind. None of his siblings were graduates and he was resolute about breaking that tradition, but Onkarmal wanted him to learn the ropes of the business. 'I couldn't sleep that night,' RK reminisces. 'As a compromise we decided I would join morning college. From 6.30 am to 9.30 am, I'd attend classes, come back home, quickly have brunch and leave for work.'

Despite his hectic schedule RK would be the first to reach the family office and stay there till evening. He also learnt French on the sides, did a correspondence course in automobile engineering, and after graduation (1958) even signed up for a year of law school, which he did not complete as the everyday grind at office gave him hands on understanding about the nuances of the legal system.

HINDUSTAN TWYFORDS LTD

Between 1955 to 1961, even while he was finishing college, RK dedicated all his energy and time in growing Rodda. But by this time the Somany family had spread its wings across various manufacturing segments from glass to textiles and ceramics. All the brothers were equal shareholders in the group, but each one was responsible for running a separate unit. Hiralal managed ceramics, Onkarmal (of Cera) and CK together ran container glass and and Surendra Kumar, who now owns Soma Textiles and Industries was given charge of the textile mills in Mumbai and Ahmadabad.

Hiralal's plan was to settle each of his brothers in a business that interested them and was by 1958 on the lookout for something else to keep RK engaged so that Lalit, the youngest brother could be initiated into business with Rodda which was a relatively small entity and a good training ground.

The idea to set up a sanitary ware plant sparked during a visit to Ranchi, where the family was building a farmhouse. Hiralal instantly realized that there was a tremendous shortage of good quality, durable earthenware for the bathrooms and if one wanted sanitary ware, only expensive imported products from Twyfords and Armitage Shanks were available in the market. Here was a prospective business waiting to be tapped!

Around this time a courtesy call to the DGTD or Directorate-General of Technical Development office (a Frankenstien monster during the License Raj that ruined the fate of many an enterprise) in Delhi, confirmed his belief that this could indeed be a viable business to get into.

A military hospital in Chennai had that year ordered 50 pieces of WCs for a new wing they were building and had been quoted an obnoxious nine month delivery period by their supplier. This incident had come to the notice of an embarrassed DGTD, which was anxious to give out a license to domestic manufacturers to collaborate with a foreign partner and get the latest technology into India.

'I insist that you bring in Vitreous China. Do it in partnership with a foreign company,' the senior industrial adivisor told Hiralal, when the two met to discuss the proposal. Encouraged by his meeting, Hiralal soon began scouting for a partnership. And in the course of this search he got in touch with Jack Hay, the Chief Executive of Twyfords.

Twyfords was a pioneer brand whose history could be traced back to the early seventeenth century, by which time the family that started it were already potters of the fifth and sixth generation. The dynasty, according to the history of the company, was founded by Joshua Twyford long before bathrooms and water closets became such an integral part of our lives.

By the mid-19th century Twyfords was a household name to reckon with and had two factories in Stoke-On-Trent in Staffordshire, from where they exported earthen ware to countries across the globe. Through numerous ups and downs the company survived and thrived and by the early 20th century, had left an indelible mark in British manufacturing and sanitation history. It went public in 1919 and by the 50s and 60s had spread its network globally, setting up production units in South Africa and Australia and building a presence in the Indian subcontinent as well.

J.R.T. or Jack Hay was heading Twyfords when the Somanys approached him for collaboration. He had spent several years as an expat and was one of the last appointees of T.W. Twyford the proprietor and a leading pioneering figure in British hygiene and sanitary ware appliances.

Jack had also spent time in India in the 1920s with the East India merchants and Hoare Miller running the Calcutta and Burmah Steam Navigation Company, and trading jute fabrics all over the world before he joined Twyfords. He knew the Somanys from his days in Calcutta and when they sought him out for a joint venture, it fit in with Twyfords' strategy of expanding their global footprint.

On the other hand, Twyfords' technical know-how on Vitreous China—an innovation they had been experimenting with since early 1930s had begun replacing earthenware by the late 1950s and would provide the Somanys with just the specifications prescribed by the DGTD. Barely a couple of years before the Somanys approached them, Twyfords had begun construction of a factory at Alsager in Cheshire that produced only Vitreous China, marking the beginnings of a phase where earthenware was being swiftly substituted.

Vitreous China, to explain in simple terms, is a material where the clay is vitrified along with a glaze and then fired jointly at very high temperatures of 1200°c. The gloss gives it a shiny finish and far higher robustness as compared with earthenware, reducing porosity significantly and improving resistance to stains, scratching and acid. Practically speaking, it is infinitely more durable than earthenware and can last several decades.

On DGTD's go ahead, Hiralal summoned his younger brother Onkarmal, who was in England at the time to buy new machinery for the glass unit in Rishra to go and have an initial meeting with Mr Hay.

The meeting went well and just a few months later, Hay along with his technical staff and company director A.J. Miller flew down to Calcutta to finalize the deal. It was decided that Twyfords would provide technical expertise, taking care of the plant over a three-year period along with the Somanys and in return, would get a 26 percent shareholding in the equity of the public company to be called Hindustan Twyfords Limited.

His only condition was that a member of the Somany family would go to England for six months to learn the nuances of the manufacturing process while work on other formalities like permits and land acquisition began in India.

'Supervision is key,' Mr Hay underlined. 'Without it you are dead in this business.' And so, no sooner had Mr Hay and his team left Calcutta, Hiralal told RK he will be the one leading a team of four people to train on the shop floor of the Twyfords plant in Stoke-on-Trent.

Somany was no engineer, merely a commerce graduate with no real understanding of machinery or chemicals. But he had a natural flair for technical subjects and while pursuing his automobile engineering correspondence course, had even tutored a dozen students on the discipline. He enjoyed working at Rodda, but wasn't instantly upset about Hiralal's diktat to hand it over to Lalit. Contrarily, he was happy at the thought of being given an opportunity to bring a sea change to the area of sanitation in the country. Majority of India in those days defecated in the open and for a large population latrines were a luxury, as Somany himself had witnessed, on his yearly trips to the native town of Chirawa in rural Rajasthan. Blending business and social commitment was an enticing proposal.

'We had to hide behind the trees to get the job done in Chirawa and there would always be the danger of snakes lurking around. I hated that,' he says. His instant reaction thus, to his brother's offer was of delight.

PASSAGE TO ENGLAND

'It's a black city,' warned Onkarmal, as RK prepared to leave for the Twyfords internship in Stoke-on-Trent, home to England's pottery industry, also commonly known as just the Potteries.

Wrote James Denley in his history of Twyfords—

'When George Bernard Shaw visited the Potteries, he gave up counting the number of chimneys in Stoke when he got to 123. Pails of black smoke hung in the air; trees, hedges, and houses were covered with soot-fall. The snow often came

down black; housewives had to choose their washdays very carefully and sometimes, when the wind was in the wrong direction, you could not see across the road from Cliffe Vale to the Fireclay.'

Shaw of course had called on much before the introduction of the tunnel kilns in the 1950s which improved life for the residents of Stoke dramatically, but the city continued to retain its dubious reputation as an industrial dump when RK and Krishna, his wife of two years reached in March 1961. He was barely 24, she much younger.

It was an adventure ride for the young couple and the team of four technicians RK was leading. It was his first time abroad and a British Airways Comet flight would take them to London. From there RK took a train and arrived at Stoke. Bags full of grocery, spices and other edibles were packed along, for the fame of Indian cuisine was yet to travel to this industrial county in the West Midlands.

On the day of his arrival, RK was informed that his accommodation would not be ready for a few weeks and so he took up boarding at the North Stafford Hotel right opposite the station. 'As per government rules, I was classified as a student, and thus was allowed only £3.5 of foreign exchange a day, whereas the hotel alone would cost £8 with no breakfast,' he laughs.

Life on the shop floor was a revelation and the lessons and skills RK learnt there held him in good stead for a long time. He got his hands dirty working across departments—as a caster, glazer, kiln man and in several other roles as part of the manufacturing process, would come back home around 6 pmI in his cotton overalls, covered in dust and grime.

Once home, he'd freshen up and as Krishna was getting dinner ready, would get his portable typewriter and take notes on the techniques he had learnt through the day. By the time of their return, he had more than 100 pages of typewritten observations that he still preserves in a vault and considers relevant even today, despite the technological advancements in the sector. 'I'd ask a lot of questions because it wasn't my area of expertise. I'd never feel any shame, because at best, someone would get irritated and walk away. But if I hadn't cleared my doubts, I could have never learnt anything. Today nobody can hoodwink me because I have my fundamentals clear,' he asserts.

Life was hard, but the officials at Twyfords took good care of their guests. Jack would call RK 'No. 5' jokingly, because he was the fifth of the six brothers. He and his wife Mary would often drop in for a meal, highly impressed by the quality, aroma, and taste of Indian spices that Mrs Somany served.

Hay had also ensured that NR Hancock, the company Director, would entertain the Somanys every other weekend, taking them to see places in the countryside. RK and his wife also enjoyed days of great tennis at Wimbledon, courtesy Twyfords. While Krishna formed a small social circle in their neighbourhood, RK joined the 'Potters Club'. Six months went by in a jiffy and before he knew, it was time to leave. Work was on full steam back in India, to get the site ready for plant, and he was needed in Delhi. On 31 August 1961, a week before he was originally scheduled to return, RK and Krishna flew back.

'The reason,' he says sheepishly, 'was that baggage rules were changing from 1 September, and I wanted to save duty on all the knick knacks, souvenirs, crockery, brocade and perfumes my wife had purchased.'

England had sure transformed the young lad from Calcutta into a gentleman. He had learnt the art of knotting a tie, keeping time, of being punctual and diligent, and under Hay's training of keeping close supervision on every nitty-gritty, every minutiae of his business. But his Baniya blood hadn't watered down evidently. Thrift and care with money, even if it was on saving customs duty, was a virtue he possessed in ample measure and this natural flair, needless to say, would come in good use when RK set out on the mission to build what was to become India's largest sanitary ware manufacturing company in the years to come.

BEGINNINGS AT BAHADURGARH

Within a week of returning to Calcutta, RK set out for Delhi. A 99-acre plot of land for the new factory had been bought at Bahadurgarh, now a bustling town on the outside edges of Delhi, often called the Gateway to Haryana. Back then it was a sleepy village with only a couple of tiny brick manufacturing units. And for several years after the Somany plant was built, life revolved around the activities of this one big factory.

Today of course the face of Bahadurgarh has changed radically with several new industries and a metro line expected to be commissioned in the next couple of years. It is one of the major cities in the national capital region (NCR).

The Bahadurgarh site was chosen because of its close vicinity to Delhi which was a key distribution hub for sanitary ware dealers in north India and also because of its proximity to Rajasthan—an important source of raw materials. RK had to push hard to get approvals for the site. Along with the sanitary ware factory, the Somanys also wanted to expand the glass business and were scouting for a location to put up a second unit.

Licenses were already given out for a piece of land in Durgapur for the Hindustan Twyfords project and Ghaziabad for the glass unit. But the brothers wanted both divisions at a single location, and getting the permit altered involved hectic lobbying with ministers and the indolent bureaucratic machinery.

'Our hands were literally tied like prisoners. From the quantum of production to the location of the factory, every bloody detail was fixed by bungling bureaucrats who had no clue about anything at all,' exclaims RK, who would over the years have to deal with such fetters on a daily basis.

He had spent a month in Delhi, trying to arrange for land clearances prior to leaving for the UK itself. The villagers were opposing the acquisition because they were fed with incorrect information that it was the Birlas who were building the factory.

'Talk of "*Birlaji ka plant aa raha hai*" spread around the community like wildfire, which meant there was an unofficial sanction to squeeze money out of us and consequently delayed construction.'

Unable to make any headway RK and Hiralal along with another company official chartered a Douglas DC-3 aircraft and went to Chandigarh to meet the then Chief Minister of Punjab (Haryana was crafted out as a separate state only by 1966), Sardar Pratap Singh Kairon.

Unlike other politicians of the day, Kairon was known to be prompt and honest in his dealings. He had famously told Nehru not to touch Punjab. 'I am a double M.A', he had bragged to Jawaharlal, making it clear to the Prime Minister that he was capable of handling the affairs of his own state and didn't want any meddling.

True to his reputation, Kairon got the job done expeditiously and even offered finance for the project. That however was unnecessary. Hindustan Twyfords Ltd had hit the capital markets with an IPO (Initial Public Offering) for 4 lakh equity shares and 20,000 preference shares. Twyfords was allotted 26 percent of equity capital equivalent to the technical know-how fee, distributing the remaining majority balance between members of the family and keeping a small percentage for the public. So staggering was the response to the issue that it was oversubscribed 78 times—a record in those days.

Construction of the plant began in April 1961, while RK was still in the UK. Before he came back, a warehouse had already been built and other than minor teething troubles, like dealing with the persistent wife of a certain minister who would harangue Somany's liaison men to send her 5 kgs of 'Burfi' every now and then in return for the co-operation her husband had extended towards the project, workers had even begun digging ground for the factory. When he returned, RK worked out of the telephone exchange building in Bahadurgarh and an office was built only from the profits the plant generated in the first two years.

'People called me *kanjoos*, but I called it frugality. A swanky office space was an extravagant expense. Even the road leading to the plant was constructed from returns and not from working capital,' he says, giving a hint into the uncanny trait among *baniyas* of all strain to save money, rather than spend it on superfluities.

Anyhow, a few months after RK's arrival, the Twyfords team led by N.R. Hancock also reached Bahadurgarh. The five-member team included Hancock, Messrs Malkin, Hulme, Lee, and Royle. They were brought in to supervise the erection, commissioning and training of the factory, which was up and running and in production just a year later. By October 1962, the first consignment, part of the pilot trials, was delivered and in March the official inauguration was presided over by Kairon, while the then chairman of ICICI, Gagan Bihari Lal Mehta, poured the first bucket of slip.

The Twyfords team was expected to stay on in India for three years, but could handover technical operations to the Indian personnel long ahead of schedule under RK's deft supervision. The plant began by manufacturing barely 60 pieces a day, but quickly scaled up to 1600 pieces by April 1963, after the shuttle kiln was commissioned. That year itself, in December, the big 405 ft tunnel kiln came into production. It was at that time the longest furnace in the world and a gentleman from the World Bank, who had come to Bahadurgarh to inspect the plant was so impressed by the state of the art facility that he couldn't stop praising young RK for his remarkable feat.

Within three years, the Bahadurgarh plant began exports to the Middle East, and countries like Ghana, Tanzania, and Kenya in Africa. In Kenya, Hindustan Twyfords soon garnered a 90 percent market share, but the Chinese moved in and spoilt the market with ridiculous pricing. China had a simple policy—prowl on export markets in order to fulfill the foreign exchange requirement of the exchequer and sell so cheap that competition would be wiped out.

'They would land their products at the prevailing domestic prices whether or not they made money. There was no point continuing, because I wouldn't even have been able to earn my sea freight or packaging costs. We eventually moved away,' says RK

Even today, in what is an hypercompetitive marketplace, where Indian and foreign sanitary ware brands have to literally jostle for space, and undercut one another to win customers, RK adheres to the simple rule of not doing business that doesn't fetch reasonable returns. That often means letting go of prestigious commercial projects (real estate condominiums, hotels, government contracts) which give volume growth but 'suck the marrow out of you'.

'Most foreign brands in the country are bleeding as a result of these practices—they quote ridiculous prices, lower even than my manufacturing cost. Let them go ahead and do it, I will concentrate on the retail side of the business and make my margin,' he says nonchalantly.

Be that as it may, what the exports business did was that it also expedited the Somany family's separation with Twyfords. In order to avoid both competition in the same markets and confusion on the source of product origin, Twyfords cashed out of its 26 percent stake four years later. The two companies parted on a good note and continued to maintain friendly relations till Twyfords was acquired by a new paper-making company called Reed International.

Not only would they rake in a profit on their investment, but Twyfords also benefitted from a reverse technology they learnt at the Bahadurgarh plant. Instead of the expensive Tin Oxide, which their plants in the UK used in the glazing process, RK had begun sourcing cheaper Zircon Opacifier and true to his thrifty ways had also asked his men to start reclaiming the overspray in the glazing process.

'It was in our blood to do something new,' says RK, 'And Twyfords could see that.' Barely a couple of years into its existence 'H-Vitreous' the rechristened brand post Twyfords' exit became a sought after household name. The high quality of their wares perceptibly stood out in the market and when Hiralal was at a dealers association meet in Chennai once, so amazed were distributors by their top notch closet that they suspected it was imported.

Dealers of Parryware, which along with Parshuram and Khodiyar were Hindustan Twyfords' key competitors, began shouting the 'Parry is dead' slogan. Parryware dominated the southern market then and continues to even today, but HTL's Vitreous China wares had managed to create such a stir among its distributors that in response to RK's onslaught, they too were forced to seek foreign collaborations to manufacture Vitreous China as their products started losing value.

'These were the very same people who had warned me saying—RK you will lose your shirt with this factory. This technology will not be accepted anywhere,' he recalls. But in no time, Parry was teaming up with the other British manufacturer Armitage Shanks and Parshuram and Kodiyar forged a JV with French company Porcher. The Seshasayees too, set up Nycer in response to this flurry of activity, getting a German collaborator.

Call it the first mover advantage, or RK's overall marketing, branding, and business acumen, 'H-Vitreous, continued to remain the market leader even after competition heated up. At one point in time it had 50 percent of the organized sanitary ware market and today 'Hindware' (the brand HSIL introduced in 1991) continues to hold 40 percent of the market, while the remainder is with various other smaller players and international brands.

Mr C.S. Gupta, a distributor of Parryware's products and someone who calls himself a silent spectator of RK's evolution as a business tycoon says one of the chief reasons why Hindware's supremacy was never meaningfully challenged in the market was because RK was a hands on shop floor man with a strong pulse of the market. He would regularly interact with dealers from all over the country to understand demand patterns, customer preferences, new designs etc to gain an edge over competition.

'He has over the years mastered the three As of marketing—availability, affordability and acceptance,' says Gupta. HSIL's brands even then had huge visibility because it had the largest distribution network in the country which now stands at 16000+ retailers and 2500 dealers. Their products were and continue to remain available in all price ranges—from low cost to ultra premium, and it has over the decades remained a widely accepted name in Indian homes, despite several other brands coming into the market as a result of its long legacy.

What also facilitated HSIL's success was RK's resolve never to say no to an order, especially if it tested his company's execution capacity and presented an opportunity for his team to learn and deliver on a challenge. 'You couldn't take Rs 10 from him if you weren't able to provide a valid enough reason for it,' says Binay Kumar, owner of the Banaras House Group, a friend of RK's and also an ex-HSIL board member about how he kept a tight check on costs. That didn't mean, however, that RK was solely money-focused. On many an occasion he took up an unviable contract purely to test his competence rather than for the pecuniary benefit that could be derived out of it.

One such occasion arose about eight or ten years ago, when out of the blue he got a call from a gentleman named Hans from Norway soliciting a meeting with him. Hans came down to Delhi a few days later with a six hundred millimetre flush vacuum closet and asked RK whether Hindware could make five hundred pieces for him of the same design and measurement in seven days. It was urgent!

Try hard as he could, RK couldn't have committed to such a proposal because neither did he have the ready moulds nor the technology for it. But he agreed to a timeframe of three months and took a token five thousand rupees as advance to finish the project.

Three months later a designer came down to inspect the consignment and rejected it on the grounds that it couldn't take a dead load of four hundred kilos for one hour. RK could have sent the man packing because such absurd specifications hadn't been discussed in the contract. But he was bent upon finishing what he had commenced and got his engineers to work nights to prepare a revised process to successfully pass the test. This was highly appreciated by the Norwegian company.

'Only when I had delivered all the pieces did I ask Hans what it was that made him contact me of all people. He said, no other manufacturer in the world had entertained his query because they felt he was being unreasonable.'

But the reason for his hurry was valid. A passenger ship was stranded at a port in Europe for the want of vacuum closets and paying astronomical damages for every extra day it spent there. A few years later when RK was travelling with his family on a Royal Caribbean cruise liner from Vancouver to Alaska, a man on the ship asked him what he did for a living?

'I build the bathroom closets you use on this ship,' RK replied with pride. It was the very ship for which RK had provided those 500 pieces several years ago.

BAHADURGARH TODAY

'The plant has seen a fifteen-fold growth from inception to date. We've done tremendous innovation over the years,' boasts one of the senior management personnel of production at the Bahadurgarh plant. He along with the general manager of the plant on site have been tasked by RK with the responsibility of showing me around the enormous facility.

It is gigantic, with a productive area of 1.5 million square feet, neatly segmented into different compartments that make up the overall manufacturing flow—perhaps the best backward integrated facility in the country. The technical experts diligently expound the fascinating, complex procedure that goes into making a simple water closet, washbasin, squat pan, or urinal that we so take for granted.

The process starts with the preparation of the slip from raw materials usually consisting of various kinds of alumina or clay, silica, and a flux like feldspar. The slip is then cast into plaster moulds of various kinds depending on the product one wants to make and a glass like glaze is usually sprayed upon the dry body to be fired in kilns. Once out after a 14 hour 'cold-to-cold' cycle in the furnace, products are labeled and checked for defects, packaged and then dispatched to dealers. It sounds simple but is ridden with a multifarious web of activities that need to be perfectly synchronized. The end to end procedure from raw material to finish takes about five days.

There are all sorts of machines, racks , storage tanks, mechanized mini rails (used for battery casting) and whirring generators on the shop floor that can bamboozle a lay onlooker, but my hosts dumb it down and explain it all in simple terms.

RK's philosophy has been to constantly modernize. The Bahadurgarh plant has seen four phases of expansion and renovation, the first of which was undertaken as early as 1967, barely five years after it was built. RK is firmly of the view that you either keep abreast with modern technology or perish and hence when he realized that the old kiln was taking 9,900 kilo calories to fire 1 kg of ware, he promptly replaced it even though he needed to borrow Rs 10 cr for the exercise. Today the same process takes only 1200 kilo calories per kilo of ware.

Similarly, there has been concerted focus on water consumption and over decades Hindware has managed to reduce the size of its water flush gradually from 15 liters to 1.5, also introducing the dual flush and aqua free flushing technologies. RK claims he is the largest manufacturer of green products and is on his way to making Bahadurgarh a zero waste plant.

His focus right from the beginning was on bringing efficiencies, whether technological, HR, or financial.

Constant trial and error has led HSIL to improve yields from 60-62 percent to 80-85 percent (pieces per 100 not sent for re-fire), while the employee head count has steadily come down from 1200 at one point to 400 as the company began progressively relying on automation and mechanization . This has been achieved even as production capacity has gone up to 1.8 million pieces per annum, which demonstrates how dramatically per capita output has shot up.

The plant's top notch in-house R&D facility, the first in this sector to be officially recognized by the government has put in a lot of effort into getting the recipe right. From tweaking raw materials to get an optimal mix, to improving schedules in order to reduce error and laboring on innovating with the glaze, body and design, RK has kept research and innovation at the epicenter of the manufacturing process not just at Bahadurgarh, but also at the other plants.

But it is his indomitable spirit and continual effort to push the boundary that keeps the energy levels high, say employees. 'He has a sharp memory. Go to him with a problem and he will give you three options, one of which has to lead you closer to the solution,' says one of the senior technical personnel. 'Every now and then he asks managers for a snapshot of what they've done and goes into the minutiae to drive his point, even though it might be a very small issue.'

'He is a quick problem solver and once he tells me to do something I know I cannot ignore it because it is half a decade of experience speaking to me,' adds another. Technicians are intimidated by his razor-sharp judgement and have often been caught off guard when he, a commerce graduate, has to give them technical instructions. One such instance happened when RK acquired Krishna Ceramics in the late 80s. He sent his technical team, headed by a senior ceramist, to the plant to take over the manufacturing process. The very next day the man called up RK with panic in his voice. 'Somany saab, the blunger has been rotating for 24 hours, but the raw material isn't getting mixed. We might have to change it'.

'Did you see if the rotation of the stator rotor is correct?' asked RK.

'You are right sir, it has been rotating in the opposite direction all along,' said he sheepishly, after inspecting the rotator.

This is common sense, you cannot buy it, says RK, recalling the incident.

But unlike other bosses who are quick to point out flaws but never appreciate initiative, RK rewards resourcefulness and isn't very harsh on employees if they err. When one of his senior technical personnel went up to him with an idea to reuse the pitcher generated from reject material, he asked him to begin work on the project with a promise that if he were was successful, the patent would be named after him.

'That inspired me to work doubly hard on it,' says he.

It took years of sheer grit and determination however for RK to bring Bahadurgarh to this plane of ingenuity and strength. A better part of his existence was spent battling, the shackles imposed by the license Raj and a hostile business climate.

WORKING THROUGH THE SHACKLES

Having seen the discipline and order of the Twyfords plant, RK had a hard time initially, reconciling to the working culture in India. Even though HSIL's products saw enormous success in the market and were flying out of the shelves in a very short span of time, it was an unsympathetic environment to do business. The labour force, largely farming folk who had never seen the insides of a factory till they stepped into the HTL plant, were his biggest headache. They would walk in for their shift several hours late and with absolute insouciance. RK began penalizing latecomers, cutting 25 paisa of their wages, but even that didn't help matters. 'They'd lob their wages on the table and say "*Saab aap hi rakh lena, aapke kaam aajayga, aaj ek beedi kum pee lenge*".'

The labour issue escalated into a full blown conflict between the management and the unions in 1965 when there was a 32 day strike. That is when RK formed a committee where both his managers as well as the union representatives would sit face to face and sort out matters. Ever since, barring a lockout once again in the late 1980s and another strike in early 2000s at the company's Bibinagar plant, which Somany had acquired in the early part of the decade, there has never been any labour trouble at HSIL.

RK used a nifty trick to ensure that his company wasn't held to ransom by labour unions. Just like the union leaders would give him a charter of demands, he too started getting his men to prepare a counter deed, setting targets on productivity, designing performance based incentives, and laying out conditions if workers wanted their demands fulfilled.

'I made it clear that there were no free lunches, and gradually things improved,' he says. 'But as long as our outdated laws are amended, labour relations will continue to remain a delicate area to tread on no matter what one does.'

The other big hitch in those days was in the way the market functioned. Dealers made a lot of money under the table selling wares at outrageously high prices and so did manufacturers by under-invoicing and later settling dues with their distributors. There was a thriving black economy. This was because the concept of indicative selling price did not exist. In order to battle this problem and make it an all-white, transparent trade, RK introduced M.R.P. long before it became a mandatory norm.

He faced an immediate backlash because dealer margins were suddenly restricted, but had an upper hand because there was a tremendous shortage of good ware in the market. In due course things stabilized because while he had capped the amount they could earn, RK continued providing dealers with decent trade margins that kept them happy.

'The minute I found out that they were selling over the M.R.P., they would be dealt with an iron fist and sacked instantly. This brought in some discipline and a great degree of transparency to a business which was chiefly conducted under the table, RK says. It also meant HSIL would earn much more than its competitors, who were losing money at the behest of errant dealers.

'Such was the demand for sanitary ware products in the mid 60s that the eight dealers who handled the Delhi market agreed to take delivery on rotation from companies because demand outstripped supply. And we would auction any extra pieces that might have been sent in the wagons among for the highest price. Even damaged pieces that were reparable would be put under the hammer,' recalls C.S. Gupta, a dealer.

His initial monopoly in the market enabled him to introduce several other such best practices. Dealers worked on a system of cash discounts which entailed payment before delivery. In practice, they would take delivery, avail the discounts but wouldn't pay for weeks on end. RK immediately brought this to an end.

While improving what was under his control, breaking through the shackles of the License Raj needed much patience and cunning. Industries were literally tied down by prescriptive and often specious and antiquated rules. Too much discretionary power wrested with corrupt officials waiting to extract their pound of flesh with every routine business transaction. Spreading ones wings out of this cage needed deft navigation of the system which RK became an expert at.

Local manufactures would be given Rs 30 for import of raw material for every hundred rupees of export. This was stated policy, but officers in the DGTD would cut down allowances at their will, paying no heed to the requirements of the plant. As a result, very often, despite high pent up demand, capacity utilization would be sub optimal as imported raw materials like ball clay, dyes, buller rings etc would be out of stock.

The DGTD office became Somany's temple. He would be relentless in his pursuit of getting work done and would reach the Directorate General's doorstep every Friday at five minutes before 3 pm for his meeting, when other proprietors were sending their managers. He'd be made to wait hours on a dirty sofa, while the peon sat opposite him scratching his head. It was only when the mandatory Rs 10 note for '*chai*' was exchanged would the file be promptly moved up.

'And it became Rs 100 during the emergency,' laughs RK. 'The higher bureaucracy was efficient, but they couldn't help you even if they wanted to because the rot began right at the level of the peon. *Neeche se file theek karvao...phir hum dekh lenge* would be their refrain.' Post liberalization, when their positions still remained but their power was effectively all but gone, the very people who had given him such grief would call upon him and say *Somaniji, chalo aaj hum aapko chai pilate hai.* Often, when it became impossible to steer through the bureaucratic morass, one had to find one's own way as RK soon learnt.

Power availability was a major issue at Bahadurgarh and would go off 20 to 30 times a day. All industrial units had to keep generators on standby in order not to disrupt activity particularly at the firing stage because if the kilns were stopped for more than five minutes, the ware would invariably develop cracks.

Hindware had a 370 KW turbo-charged generator manufactured by the English Electric Company which broke down one day. As luck would have it, RK was in England at the time and got a panic call from his manager asking him whether certain spare parts of the turbo charger could be imported. Import of something even as small as a 40 pound turbo charger part would have needed authorization from the DGTD. Going through the official channel involved the long procedure of applying for a license which could have taken several months. RK couldn't have stalled work for so long—he would have gone out of business. The only option was to smuggle the parts into India. He bought a brand new Samsonite office bag, put the piece into it and walked through the green channel casually.

Luckily he wasn't caught.

That very engine would work 24/7, when the opening of the floodgates during the war with Pakistan in 1971 caused large scale non availability of power for six months. 'The basic endeavor of the socialist leaning government machinery,' he says 'was to make life as inconvenient for businessmen as possible.'

HSIL at the start had a license to manufacture 5,400 metric tons of sanitary ware annually. One year, because of increased efficiency, the company inadvertently crossed this limit. All hell broke loose. The DGTD hauled up Somany questioning why the company crossed the licensing limit. 'Which other country penalized the spirit of enterprise? So when the National Productive Council once sent us manufacturers a circular asking whether the DGTD should continue, I wrote in their four-page form saying it should promptly be dismantled because it wasn't the Directorate General of "Technical Development" but of "Total Destruction",' he chuckles heartily.

It is through such bureaucratic quagmire that HSIL steadily grew and today manufactures 7.2 sanitary ware pieces a minute, 433 every hour and 3.8 million every year, making it the largest sanitary ware brand in the country. It has been recognized as amongst the top 300 companies in India and was rated by *Forbes* magazine amongst the top 100 small and medium sized companies in India.

LIBERATION, DIVERSIFICATION & THE BIG SPILT

Nearly twenty years after the construction of the Bahadurgarh plant, HSIL did its first diversification, expanding into container glass manufacturing through the acquisition of Associated Glass Industries Ltd.

It was a moribund Private Public Partnership undertaking which was closed down. The owner would wile away time at the Secundarabad Club spending upwards of Rs 1 lakh rupees a month on company account rather than look at salvaging the fortunes of his business which was panting for breath.

Hindustan National Glass was by then the country's top container glass manufacturer, looked after jointly by CK and Onkkarmal, but HSIL was the most profitable entity in the Somany empire. So when APIDC approached them with an offer to take it over, it was decided by the family that the buyout would happen through HSIL. 'We were making tons of profit and paying heavy taxes. This plant came to us literally free, because under rule 72-A of the Income Tax Act, we could offset the tax component of HSIL with losses arising out of the amalgamation with AGIL,' says RK, explaining the rationale for the buyout.

Over the next few years RK and his nephews, who were then looking after the plant, concentrated all their might in turning it around. It was literally a basket case—electricity was a major problem, labour unrest and violence a recurring theme (which led to a six month lockout being declared in 1983). The plant was severely mismanaged at all levels and took several years to bring it back to health.

Nearly all six hundred employees at the unit had been engaged in low-quality cut glass production, where phosphorous was used instead of lead, which results in the glass looking lacklustre. RK realized this, and immediately closed that division down. He also upgraded both the furnaces, introducing latest temperature control electronic systems. Extensive kiln repairs and machinery upgradation works were also taken up simultaneously and within five months assembly lines were resumed and the plant began producing more glass than specified by its erstwhile Hungarian collaborators. Sure enough, in under a year, the company swung back to life, but acute power shortages and the 1983 lockout once again sent operations into a tailspin.

It was only by 1988, by which time ample money and time had been poured into modernizing the unit, enhancing production capacity by applying for new licenses and a new highly energy efficient, automated furnaces constructed, that operations stabilized. But it wasn't until post 1996, the year the Somany brothers split their empire that this plant made any significantly money.

Today, it has undergone several facelifts including four phases of reconstruction that Sandip, RK's son undertook in 2000, 2004, 2009, and 2013, and is the largest bottling unit in South India catering to marquee names in the fizzy drinks category and alcoholic beverages segments such as Coca Cola, Pepsi, Sab Miller etc. Renamed AGI Glasspac, it has a capacity to produce 1643 million pieces per annum including 953 million bottles at the Bibinagar facility and 690 million pieces at the second container glass manufacturing facility at Bhongir, Andhra Pradesh. HSIL holds 16 percent of the container glass market in the country and the glass division on the whole contributes to nearly 45 percent of the company's bottom-line.

In 1989, RK also expanded inorganically when Krishna Ceramics Ltd, a sanitary ware manufacturing unit in Bibinagar was put up on sale. It was acquired and amalgamated into the HSIL fold to cater to the southern market, immediately facilitating a 10 percent increase in the company's market share. A decade later he also bought Raasi Ceramics from India Cements to further expand sanitary ware capabilities. It was a dilapidated unit and too much money would have had to be spent on renovating it, so the plant was shuttered but the brand was retained, with part production being outsourced to an outside contractor.

While he was expanding his own companies, RK was also instrumental in building the glass and tile factories his brothers ran and the Soma Plumbing tap-making plant in Sahibabad, which his nephew, Shreekant Somany was to look after. Equally, his brothers were a solid pillar of support for RK through and through, and it was only as a result of this mutual give and take that each of them could flourish in their own lines of business.

But by the early 90s, as India opened its gates to foreign investors, lifting most restrictions on businessmen with the liberalization of its economy, the four surviving brothers (Onkarmal and Lalit had passed away by then) sat down and decided it was in their best interest to divide the empire. At any rate each one's, role and area of business had been clearly demarcated by Hiralal right at the onset, and it was felt that with the second generation entering the family fold, every brother and his family must have the autonomy to grow his business without restriction to avoid any future conflict.

PricewaterhouseCoopers was given the mandate to draw up the broad contours of the split. It was decided that each brother would retain the business he had been running all these years (or pay a 15 percent premium to buyout another's, an option that none chose to exercise) and sell his shareholding in the other companies in order to divide the empire into four separate entities—ceramics for Hiralal, sanitary ware for RK, container glass (barring the AGI facility) for CK, and Soma Textiles for Surendra Kumar.

Based on what valuation each of these units garnered,

the brothers would also have to pay off one another in order to equalize the value of the deal. Here's where the troubles began. CK who was supposed to pay a large sum of money to RK in lieu of the HNG shares that RK had sold to him, didn't stick to his word.

'You have no faith in me?' he blared, and stormed out red faced saying he had no intentions of discussing the matter further, when RK went to ask for the money. An option to pay a reduced amount was also discussed, but the dues haven't been settled till date. He doesn't dwell too much on the past though. 'God has been more than generous with me,' RK says. 'I can't eat more than one *roti* at a time, can I?'

The incident did however firm up his conviction, that it was in everyone's interest to keep business strictly separate from family—a line of thought not many family run *Baniya* businesses will agree with. 'Not in seven life times will I allow a relative—with the exception of my son Sandip, and grandson Shashwat—in the company,' he asserts. 'And thank god I have only one son, and two married daughters, who've been well provided for by their families and by me, so succession planning isn't something that gives me sleepless nights either,' he adds.

PASSING THE BATON

The fact that Sandip, RK's son would one day enter the family business was an underlying assumption that didn't need highlighting. Like all his other cousins, he too came into the

HSIL fold way back in 1982 as a trainee after studying ceramic manufacturing technology at the University of California and had an extensive induction period for three years, in which just like his dad, he spent time roving from department to department understanding diverse processes.

In the initial years he was a key member of the team that undertook a critical modernization and expansion program of HSIL's plants and subsequently under RK's guidance, swiftly took the company to soaring heights. Several positive factors converged to make this possible.

Sandip's first decade at HSIL was spent observing how the internal dynamics of a family run business worked. And while he was often bursting with ideas, he was curtailed by the firm grasp his uncle Hiralal had over the smallest of decisions. With utmost candor, Sandip reveals that even though RK was the top boss at HSIL, Hiralal the elder brother as group chairman of the Somany empire was a dominating patriarch, and functioned with the autocracy of a military commander, even though his intentions were always well meaning. RK had tremendous respect for his brother who was almost like a father figure and so would rarely question his decisions even if they jarred.

'He was 18 years senior to my father and so it was a no questions asked relationship,' says Sandip, who began to feel claustrophobic in this environment. He remembers an instance where the family had got permissions to set up a cement manufacturing unit in Madhya Pradesh in the 1980s, but Hiralal decided they wouldn't go ahead with the proposal because the cement business would one day garner such tremendous scale that one of the four brothers running it would get an unfair advantage over the other three.

Such kind of myopia coupled with a very micro-managerial approach to running a business, was unnerving and so when the spilt happened in 1995, it was a god send for Sandip, who was waiting to spread his wings. HSIL had been liberated from two ends—by the government in 1991 and from the constraints of joint family ownership four years after.

'That is the year I came into my own,' says Sandip, for whom hard work and long hours weren't an alien concept. He'd seen his dad spend twelve hours a day at the factory and soon enough that became his routine too, as he got down to readying his company to take on the challenges of a free market.

RK gave him enough autonomy to do things his own way even though their personalities were like chalk and cheese. Sandip's go-getter, aggressive nature was just what was needed to break out of the old approach. Barely a year after the split in 1996, HSIL celebrated its big milestone of crossing Rs 100 cr in revenues and in under twenty years it almost touched a topline of Rs 2000 cr.

A lot of hard work has gone into making it what it is. The initial challenge was that of defending itself against the onslaught of foreign competitors as well as maintaining its lead over domestic players. This required a radical shift in the way business was traditionally conducted and among the first significant changes Sandip introduced was a decentralized leadership structure, to speed up decision-making. Vertical heads were bought in for all key functions so that RK and Sandip could spend their time strategizing rather than pouring over minutiae of sales figures.

He also spent a lot of time on product innovation, drilled it into his personnel that their approach would have to be more consumer-centric rather than plant-centric. This meant sanctioning larger budgets for improved capabilities, state of the art machinery and technology in order to cater to what the consumer wanted instead of what the plant could produce. A rebranding exercise was carried out first in 2004 and again in 2011 to make the brand more youthful and global in appeal.

The initial years proved to be a good breathing period for the company to get its act together and face up to the rapid pace of change that was about to hit them by the 2000s. Many legacy family businesses had rushed to diversify into unrelated businesses post 1991 when the restrictions were lifted. But because of the separation, RK didn't have much money for any trial and error and with hindsight that proved to be a blessing in disguise. Both Sandip and he concentrated their full capacity on revitalizing the existing business for the boom of the new century, rather risk their reputation elsewhere.

They took baby steps rather than big strides, acquiring small plants like the Havel's India's bath fittings business to get into faucet manufacturing, or a stake in PET bottle manufacturer Garden Polymer more recently in the glass division. The cautious approach helped steer clear of any major blips or problems of over leverage that sent many a tycoon knocking at the BIFR's doors.

What Sandip also did was segmented the market much more distinctively catering to a range of budgets with the Hindware, Hindware Art and Luxury Hindware Italian collections, and gradually diversified the business from being a mere sanitary ware brand to a complete home solutions provider. Today HSIL manufactures faucets and bath fittings and is expanding its capacity in this line with a plant that's coming up in Gujarat. What it doesn't make, HSIL imports or trades in, through foreign joint ventures, and collaborations for things like ceramics, tiles, kitchen appliances and wellness products.

With Evok—the retail brand which Sandip's wife manages, the company entered the lifestyle accessories categories. With 17 stores, the brand is still not making profits, but the expectation is that it should become lucrative in the next couple of years.

For a company that for decades produced and sold just 10-12 items, Hindware today has hundreds of designs, variations and options in its catalogue—a reflection of how dramatically the market has changed.

'We've gone from being a maker of utilitarian products, to a company that makes products people aspire for. The perception around this category has changed completely and there is now a growing emphasis on luxury.' The plan going ahead is to concentrate on retail and distribution of B-to-C branded categories says Sandip, rather than expanding the manufacturing lines at least till the business climate improves.

HSIL has seen a compounded annual growth rate of 20 percent in net sales and EBITDA and Sandip is confident that his company is poised to see a 25 percent growth in both topline and bottomline in the next decade, by which time it will be time for Shashwat, RK's grandson to get into business (if he wants to that is, adds Sandip).

'He won't be accepted just because he is the boss's son. We will make sure he goes through the same grind that both my father and I did.'

A FULL LIFE

It has taken RK single-minded devotion to his profession to reach where he has. At 77, he still has an eighteen-hour day that begins at 6.30 am in the morning and finishes only by the stroke of midnight, when he retires to his room. The time in between is interspersed with meetings, frequent day trips outside Delhi, and a myriad social commitments. He only took one day off last year when he fell ill, and so itchy was he at home, that in the afternoon he went back to office.

It has been a dynamic life full of vitality. Apart from the new scales he's managed to take HSIL to, he has held numerous positions of responsibility serving many federations and industry lobbies. He was chairman of the Council of Indian Employers, President of the Employers' Federation of India, President of the Associated Chambers of Commerce and Industry (ASSOCHAM), President of the PHD Chamber of Commerce and Industry and continues to remain an active member of the Rotary Club of Delhi Mid Town.

His colleagues say he is a keen observer and silent listener and has been instrumental in setting the benchmarks for Indian sanitary ware standards, aligning them to global best practices, helping bodies like the BIS (Bureau of Indian Standards) develop their own blueprints. They call him the *Bhishma Pitamah* of sanitary ware for his immense contribution to the field. His mantra has always been to give what he embarks on his full one hundred percent, never leaving a job unfinished.

'In the past 50 years that I've been a member of Rotary, I haven't missed a single meeting,' he tells me proudly. 'From Singapore to London and Paris to various locations across America, I've made it a point to attend all meetings, no matter which part of the world I am in. All it takes is a minute to refer to the Rotary directory and find out the location of the club closest to you.'

And why such commitment to an activity that most other members are so flippant about? 'It is my passion to meet new people and learn one new thing every day,' he says. But somewhere, it is also a challenge he has set for himself, one reckons, to not break his own record. He has tremendous willpower and once something is decided, it is written in stone. He couldn't live without *papad*, so one day he decided to give it up for one year. Similarly he hasn't had an ice cream or a cola for the last 22 years to test his self-control. No surprise then that he is among those rare breed of people who've managed to reverse diabetes.

Even the worst of personal tragedies haven't been able to dampen his indomitable spirit, say his children. In 1975, RK lost his first wife Krishna. No one knows what happened. She fell in the bathroom, hurt her head and before he could reach Calcutta from Bahadurgarh to meet her in the hospital, she was pronounced dead.

A year later, he married again and in barely six days, Lata, his second wife died of a massive heart attack. It took him years to come out of the shock, but at the insistence of his mother and sister-in-law, in 1977, RK tied the knot again with Snehlata, with whom he had a happy marriage for 23 years till 2000, when whilst in China he learnt that she too had passed away. 'She had an intuition, because just the night before she died, she had called up all her loved ones across the country,' he recalls.

Between building an empire and bringing up three children—Sandip, Sandhya, and Divya, RK could have lapsed into a severe depression with such setbacks, but he took it on his chin and moved on. He had strong familial support and importantly work was his therapy. 'He was a hands-off father, but never an absentee father,' says Sandhya. 'He knew of our whereabouts, our school schedules and grades and I remember him reprimanding me a little when I got home with terrible marks in math. "*Marwari ki beti hoke itne bure marks, he scolded!*"'

Sandhya would like him to slowdown but he refuses to. 'He yearns for work even on holidays,' she says. 'He sets deadlines for himself on a book he must read or paperwork he must complete, and these are written in stone, no matter that he is accountable to no one. That's how high he sets the bar for himself.'

After Sandip took over as the joint managing director and grew the company to a far higher scale than he could have imagined, RK consciously decided to step aside from the day-to-day running of the business to work on the broader vision for HSIL , to look at policy matters on areas as wide ranging as sexual harassment to whistleblower protection and keep a closer vigil on compliance in order not to be caught on the wrong side of SEBI/listing agreements.

But it is impossible to get the spirit of the factory floor man out of him, says Sandip, disagreeing with RK's own assessment of his role in the company. No matter that the scale HSIL has acquired today (two sanitary ware facilities, two glass manufacturing units, two units to produce faucets and two for PET bottles) doesn't practically allow him to get his hands dirty, he still tries to keep his ear close to the ground, crisscrossing the country to visit his various plants and ensure his work doesn't begin and end at the corner office.

'I should normally be the operations guy and he the visionary setting long-term goals, going aggressively after M&A, but he still loves being a plant-centric manager who is completely involved in solving the problem of the day.'

But if he had to enter business today, he wouldn't get into manufacturing if they paid him for it proclaims RK. 'The license permit Raj has given way to the police Raj, the business climate is terrible, labour laws are outdated and you can no longer get land,' he says, echoing the concerns of several in corporate India.

All these challenges however don't weigh him down, and he'd rather tackle them head on than hang up his boots. 'Not until I die,' cries RK, when I ask him if he will retire soon. There is far too much work to get done before he can call it a day.

His current pet project is one he's undertaken as Chairman—Governing Body of the Indian Plumbing Skills Council. Along with NSDC which has sanctioned Rs 5 cr, RK and a few others have put in their own money in a national level program to train 12,000 trainers, who in turn will be required to train and certify 1.2 million more plumbers in the next ten years.

His motivation to chair this project was the simple realization that 95 percent of defects in sanitary ware products were as a result of bad installation and plumbing, and not because of an inherent fault in the product itself. This in turn is because a majority of the workforce in the plumbing industry is not professionally trained. 'I want this project to succeed,' he says. 'I also want to see women plumbers in my lifetime. There is one plumber in Pune who owns a Renault Duster, because he is so successful in his profession. He inspires me,' he says with a childlike animation in his voice.

He says he'd like to do more in the field of women's education. The school owned by the Somany family in native Chirawa celebrated 100 years in 2012 and RK continues to be actively involved in the administration of the college the family runs there. He built a separate wing for girls around a decade ago when he realized they weren't attending classes because it was a co-ed set up. And nothing gives him more pleasure than to see young women flocking in the campus in their mopeds and Maruti-800s.

'That is a sign of empowerment. Do you know why the drop-out ratio of girls is so high in our country? It is because of lack of sanitation,' he says, narrating to me case after case to drive his point about why good sanitation should be at the center of everything we do.

Any regrets, or unfulfilled ambitions, I ask as we wind down for the evening. 'I don't dwell on the past, or have time for regrets,' he states, and tells me instead about his one yet to be realized dream.

'Ever since I can remember, I had dreamt of buying a Rolls Royce and a Jaguar. I've bought both. What I wish for now is to get my hands on a beautiful vintage jalopy which I can sit with my tools and repair.'

It's a small dream of a big man, but his is a legacy of humility. Also of determination and tremendous hard work backed up by the shrewdness and sagacity—essential to plot a course ridden with difficulties. With Sandip, RK has a worthy heir, who over the last 30 years that he's been in business has proved that despite their contradictory styles of functioning, it is their shared moral fibre on ideas of transparency, integrity, and market reputation which will provide a continuum to HSIL even as the baton is passed on from one generation to another.

COACH

V.K. Bansal - Bansal Classes

Half an hour before the Golden Temple Express approaches the station, a gentleman gets into the AC-1st compartment. He promptly manages to draw the attention of the stern looking Shambhu Agrawal, his wife and their IIT aspirant teenage son. The foursome engage in what appears like a long and serious conversation about the best IIT coaching institute in town. Copious amount of information is parted with, several eminent establishments summarily derided by the gentleman and one name in particular is propped as being the only place to go to. As the train pushes past Dakaniya Talav station, he begins helping the family unload their luggage and along with *namastes* and smiles of gratitude, phone numbers are exchanged so that the Agrawals can 'call anytime if further help is needed'.

Little has the unsuspecting family guessed that the smooth talking, (if persuasive) man wasn't merely a knowledgeable co-passenger eager to help. Or that he could've been, as one suspected after spending three days making sense of the phenomenon that is this town, a disguised sales agent appointed by one of the many hundred institutes here with a two-fold purpose to push their own establishment and bad mouth competition.

If heavy duty marketing of the most vicious kinds has begun long before the train grinds to a halt at the platform, the fight for students—the town's lifeline—only gets more hectic as the noisy auto rickshaw paces with frenzy, traversing the dusty roads that are lined up with hoarding after another advertising coaching for IIT JEE, AIEEE, and Pre-Medical. Even the auto rickshaw driver comes with a mandate to publicize one or the other institute!

And boy there are many! As we cross the unadorned (by hoardings) cantonment area and speed towards Madhushree Hotel in Talawandi, the visual assault gets fiercer. The billboards become bigger and flashier and a group, whose mugs wouldn't otherwise appear on hoardings in any other town in India or abroad, begin making their presence felt. Teachers—this town's rock stars—look out of these hoardings. 'B.K.M. Sir', 'S.A. Sir' et al. Their CVs listing out their proud backgrounds—'ex-Bansal'—and prouder achievements—'captured top ranks—AIR 5th (general catagory) in 2007, AIR-141 in AIPMT in 2012, AIR-22 in JEE in 2009. Also smiling down posters are students—'Stars of Turning Point', 'Rajasthan topper—GEE Advanced Chitrang Murdia'.

So on and so forth.

This is Kota—India's coaching capital, thronged every year by lakhs of prospective students wanting to pursue engineering or medicine. They leave home in Mumbai or Madurai, Delhi or Dalhousie, Varanasi or Valsad, to study at Bansal, Allan, Vibrant, Resonance, Career Point, EduWave, Akash, and Etoos. Or scores of other smaller coaching institutes that have mushroomed at every corner in this town, on the banks of the Chambal, promising to facilitate that grand dream of cracking the IIT or medical entrance.

Kota was once Rajasthan's Industrial capital. It's chemical, fertilizer and synthetic fiber units putting it prominently on the nation's industrial map. And it continues to remain an important hub, being home to the factories of DCL, Shriram Fertilizers & Chemicals, Chambal Fertilizers & Chemicals, Instrumentation Ltd etc. But, coaching is today the core of its identity.

Students fuel Kota's fire. Aside of the Rs 80,000 spent on coaching fees, living expenses per head per annum are in the region of Rs 100,000 to Rs 150,000. A conservative average of Rs 200,000 per student and we are talking of a Rs 2,000 cr annual stimulus for this town, which in many ways rose like the proverbial phoenix from the ashes when its leading industrial house J K Synthetics shuttered its plant in the late 1990s.

And the one man responsible for steering this ascent was Vinod Kumar Bansal or 'Bansal Sir'. His is a story of triumph through the worst kind of adversity, the story of a man who despite his debilitating disease which restricted him to a wheel chair all his life, gave mobility to thousands of young Indians as he helped them realize their dreams.

BECON OF LIGHT

V.K. Bansal was born in Jhansi on 26 October 1949. His arrival in a sense offered a beacon of light to his parents. The family lived in such abject poverty that his father Bishamber Dayal couldn't even afford electricity for the house. The boy would study in the dim light of a kerosene lantern, the smoke stinging his eyes. So, very early on, his mission became to bring light to his home.

When VK was barely a toddler, Bishamber shifted his family to Lucknow. His grandfather Jagannath Prasad owned a small halwai shop in Jhansi, but the income from that was scarcely enough to sustain the livelihoods of all his sons. So when VK's father got a job in the UP Irrigation Department as a low division clerk, he was promptly dispatched to Lucknow, where the family finally settled in a very modest dwelling in Daliganj.

'The rent was Rs 22, but unlike the homes of our neighbours, we did not have electricity at home. One fine Sunday morning, I went up to *Babuji* and asked him why we too couldn't get a bulb. He merely smiled and said we certainly can.'

'But when *Babuji*?' I asked,' remembers VK.

'Soon. Just work towards it. Study hard, stay focused and get a scholarship, so we can use that money to buy it.'

The answer had a profound impact on VK. The little boy of six assumed it was because of his lack of effort that the family was being deprived of electricity. So what began was more or less a contractual obligation, with VK vowing to put in all his effort into academics so that one day he could light up his home.

He began studying in all earnest, impressing teachers with his dedication at the local Shri Durga Geeta Vidyalaya, a Hindi medium school that he attended till class 10. In class six he stood first, receiving a scholarship of Rs 60, and repeated this feat in class seven as well when the amount increased to Rs 72. Every year thereafter, he topped class and by the end of class ten he had collected a total Rs 370 in scholarship money.

Bishamber promptly went to the market, purchased two bulbs and one table fan. That day still remains vividly etched in VK's memory. 'Looking back, I realize what a great way it was to motivate me. By leaving me with no choice but to do well if I wanted a bulb, my father made sure academic excellence became a necessity not an option.'

Unquestionable integrity was another virtue VK imbibed from his *babuji*. As a clerk in a government office there was ample opportunity to make money on the sides. But Bishamber wasn't a man easily tempted by inducements.

'On completion of his first month in office, an envelope containing Rs 26 made its way to his desk. His superintendent asked him to 'enjoy', but my father was furious. He promptly handed it back to his boss and told him there was no question of accepting any unsolicited envelopes hereon,' remembers VK. 'He believed greatly in the philosophy of karma and when the son of a dishonest chief engineer in his department died in a plane crash he related the incident to the corruption the man was involved in.

It was in this sort of morally righteous background—where dishonesty, lethargy or any vice for that matter was strictly forbidden that VK finished school. Such was the moral influence his father exerted on the boy, that till date he lives life by the simple tenets he was taught by the man.

'Even though I faltered a little during college, the resolve to never let go of my basic integrity was literally injected into the blood by my father,' says VK. And no matter that he is a renowned mathematics tutor today, honesty is the first lesson he teaches his students when they come from every nook and corner of the country to learn at his institute in Kota.

That is also the founding principal on which he built his business. 'It was the easiest thing for me to been dishonest in this trade, but if I earned Rs 100, I paid Rs 30 as tax and I still do,' claims Bansal, who at one point was the highest income tax payer in the Kota jurisdiction. When the tax commissioner asked him to pay only a third of the amount, give him a share and keep the rest by showing false expenditure, he told the gentleman that a disabled person couldn't possibly show the tax office that he was kicking up his heels in Europe or going to the cabaret on company account. The stunned man bid a quiet exit.

FREEDOM

If childhood was a righteous period of academic diligence, college was a small hiatus during which VK truly breathed a debauched, happy-go-lucky existence of revelry and fun.

Taking his studiousness and aptitude for academics into consideration VK was shifted out of Shri Durga Geeta Vidyalaya after class 10 to Christian College, from where he would pass out with a distinction in all subjects. He stood 15th in Uttar Pradesh, a marvelous achievement given 5-6 lakh students had sat for their class 12 higher secondary board exams that year.

Bishamber had for long nurtured an ambition to see his son pursue an MSc Physics degree. Back in the day postgraduates from the physics stream would get jobs that paid Rs 300-500 per month and so it was more or less decided for VK that he would be admitted into a good college in Lucknow after the boards and chase his father's dream.

His *Tauji* or elder uncle however would have none of it and put his foot down. 'He is a brilliant chap and he must be given an opportunity to become an engineer,' *Tauji* told a disgruntled Bishamber.

Engineering was a pipe dream for him, perhaps because as a low rung government official in the state irrigation department, he was conditioned to believe that it was a profession meant only for the *badasahibs*, not an aspiration a common man could harbor.

'I won't be able to manage the fees *bhaisaab*,' he told VK's uncle.

'If you aren't able to, I will take care of it,' said *Tauji*, putting Bishamber in a tight spot. He didn't want to be under any monetary obligation, but neither could he disregard his elder brother's wish. Eventually, he gave in.

Without further ado a letter was sent to a cousin who lived in Baneras asking for the BEnCO (Benaras Engineering College now IIT-BHU) application form to be dispatched by speed post. VK sat with his animated *Tauji* and filled the form and within days got a letter saying he had been accepted on the engineering program.

There was jubilation in the house and the worry lines on Bishamber's forehead were instantly wiped out because VK was one of the seventeen students selected on a scholarship scheme for boys who were both meritorious and needy. It was called the MCM—merit cum means scheme. Not only were his tuition fees waived off, but he was also to get a stipend of Rs 75 per month, which would partially take care of his lodging and boarding charges.

With the burden of duty off his shoulders, now that his father wasn't sending money from home, a new carefree V.K. Bansal was born at Banaras. The docile, studious boy from Lucknow suddenly transformed into a college brat in the company of a colorful set of friends who occupied room numbers 10, 9 and 8, adjacent to his 11th room, which he shared with Arun Singhal from Muzzaffarnagar.

'I gambled, smoked, got drunk, played *taash* and indulged

in every other vice apart from prostitution for which Benaras was famous,' recounts VK. He remembers raucous drunken soirées spent gambling with friends.

'We would literally bathe in alcohol,' he laughs.

Rich boys from renowned schools like Doon and Don Bosco became his friends. Most were sons of industrialists with scant worry about the future. But VK's circumstances were quite different. He may have been a merit holder, but it was still incumbent upon him to make the most of his years in college and find a well paying job to support the family at the end of four years. Alas, he got carried away by their care-a-damn attitude, paying little attention to academics till one day Bishamber sniffed that his son was up to more mischief than was desired.

'In the third year of college, my performance plummeted. I got 68 percent, which was a big comedown for someone who had always topped his class.' VK was at home when the results came and he deployed all forms of brazen chicanery to ensure his mark sheet wouldn't reach the doorstep. He even thought of bribing the university clerks, but before he could do that Bishamber got hold of the post.

VK was promptly summoned to the room. He distinctly remembers the scene. 'I was petrified because those were days in which it was considered standard for an enraged father to slap a son or hurl a chappal at his face. But *babuji* did nothing of the kind. All he told me was—"Vinod, when I depart this world, I will leave behind one rusted iron trunk in which there will be two *phati banians* (torn vests), one for you and the other for your younger brother. Be willing to accept this as your sole inheritance or do something meaningful with your life. You have a chance to take your career to the sky or throw it in the bin, think about the choice you want to make. For now, get out of the room".'

So grave was the warning, and solemn Bishamber's tone that VK felt he'd much rather have been smacked. Nonetheless, it proved to be a turning point in his college life. Quietly, without making his effort too conspicuous to his friends, he began working at his books. He set an internal goal for himself to silently achieve such astounding academic success, that it would create the loudest clamor in the university.

His will triumphed. He topped his fifth year and on the basis of his results for all four years, he stood third in the university, leaving his friends and professors to wonder how the notorious chap managed the feat. 'Today, from firsthand experience I tell my students that every child has infinite capability. It is up to each one to decide how much of it must be put to good use.'

LULL BEFORE THE STORM

In 1971, almost immediately after he graduated, VK got placed in the Kota-based plant of JK Synthetics—run by India's then third largest business house, the Singhania group. JK had installed its first manmade fiber unit in 1962 and was looking for fresh engineers to work on a new polyester filament yarn expansion project. It wasn't exactly the most favorable time for employment seekers and many of VK's batch mates were scrambling to find work. Nepotism and connections played a big role in landing a good job, but mercifully the chief engineer at the JK plant had vowed to induct only toppers that year and VK was selected on merit. He was amongst the rare candidates perhaps in that period of economic turmoil to have been offered two jobs.

He had rejected an offer from Machine Tools Corporation in Ajmer and come to Kota instead. On 31 October 1971, he began work as assistant engineer at JK. Bishamber was very clear that his son should join a private limited company, fatigued as he was by the moribund, unproductive environment of the public sector in which he had spent all his vital years.

'He even tore up a form I had procured for the UPSC entrance exam because he was dead against government jobs. *Aatma kali hoti hai*, he would say in Hindi.'

In Kota, the young VK found lodging in a room on the first floor of a small independent house near Mohan Talkies, in the town's Sabzi Mandi area. The rent was Rs 20 a month because the room didn't have a door and he was happy to save up, making do only with a curtain at the doorframe till he got his official quarters in J.K. Nagar. His salary of Rs 525 per month could have afforded a better dwelling, but years of austerity didn't mentally permit him to be a wastrel.

The initial years at JK were charming. In a few months the company allotted him with a house in the colony—SQB 13. Assistant engineers worked in eight hour shifts, and there was ample free time to while away at the colony club where VK would play billiards, table tennis, and *aaplu*, a card game he got all his colleagues addicted to. For the first time in his life he could sense a feeling of comfort and security, the kind that financial independence brought to someone who had been chained to poverty all his life.

Two years passed by in a whiz and just as the young engineer was settling to a carefree life of ease, a letter summoning him home arrived. VK's grandfather in Jhansi had picked a bride for him and he was called back home for the engagement. 'I wasn't even allowed to meet her,' he recalls with amusement. 'My grandfather had made the decision, and his word was sacrosanct.'

But VK being the adventurous boy that he was convinced his grandmother to hatch a ploy so as to ensure he could catch a glimpse of his bride to be before the wedding day. She reluctantly agreed, and took her grandson to Neelam's house from the back lane under the pretext of meeting his mother-in-law. There, over tea VK stole a glance at Neelam, barely looking up for a split second, when his veiled wife handed him the teacup.

Life got even better after marriage. He had a companion to share his home with and the young couple spent many a wonderful months together at SQB 13, in company of other newlyweds and VK's colleagues and friends who like him resided in the comforting bonhomie of quiet colony life.

Until that one day, when their life would literally be torn apart.

LIFE, UPTURNED

A pleasant Sunday morning in late 1974—VK felt a terrible weakness in his muscle as he tried to lift his body and get up after sitting cross legged in the porch. Only after he pressed the floor hard with his finger could he move. It was a dreadful feeling and intuitively even though the incident wasn't meaningful enough to cause panic, he felt something horrible was happening to him.

A local doctor—Dr A.Q. Khan at Kota's CMH Hospital was consulted immediately. All he told VK was that he was suffering from an elementary muscular disorder and it would be advisable to seek further help at AIIMS, Delhi so that a more precise diagnosis of the condition could be arrived at.

VK got back home in a state of anxiety. He summarily wrote to his uncle Dr Ramesh Dayal, a PhD in Botony at the Forest Research Institute, Dehradun and requested him to reach Delhi at once to accompany him to the hospital.

The suspense about what exactly was happening to him lingered on for longer than expected. The doctors at AIIMs performed a muscle biopsy, did various blood tests and arrived at a dual judgment—either biocitis or muscular dystrophy, before they finally concluded that it was the latter. 'Your muscles have started to decay and the degeneration process will aggravate gradually. It is a genetic disorder with no cure, you will live to see 40 at best,' the doctor proclaimed.

VK's world came crashing down. The doctor's words reverberated through his head as he stepped out of the AIIMs building with his teary-eyed uncle. As the reality sank in bit by bit, his response to it went from shock to self-pity to worry and finally to disbelief. This can't happen to me, he thought as he took Neelam, who expedited her return from Jhansi to join him in Delhi to see the Qutub Minar. He wanted things to seem as normal as possible to her.

But their routine thereafter was anything but normal. What started was a concentrated effort to seek help from every nook and corner of the country to see whether anybody had a miracle cure. Bishamber took him to the Ayurvedic Institute of Medical Sciences in Kerala, where for a month he underwent rigorous sessions until they told him they could only give him symptomatic treatment and not much else. A homeopath in Agra, a specialist in Delhi, myriad doctors in Kota, nobody could work their magic. If anything, a Meerut physician's wrong treatment exacerbated the decay and his condition worsened quicker than it would have had he not consented to the operation. VK would now walk with a visible limp.

It was in the course of these grueling years that Pooja, Aarti, and Sameer were born in 1975, 1978, and 1979 respecively. If these events should ordinarily have been a cause of celebration for the family, for VK they only meant additions to an already burgeoning list of responsibilities that he'd have to discharge in what was a race against time.

'You will live to see 40 at best,' the doctor's words constantly echoed in his head. And the only other thing that played on his mind was that he must find an additional source of income to build a kitty that would secure his family's future before departing this world. This unease was further fed by the fact that he'd had a fall in the factory one day and in his subconscious veered the possibility that he would be sacked. All this made him constantly irritable and at the receiving end of his anger would be his wife.

'He'd want to help with the kids, let them play on his lap and because he couldn't do it, he would get irritated at the smallest things,' remembers Neelam, who would be simultaneously feeding one child, getting the homework of another done, while trying to calm the third wailing baby, alongside dealing with her husband's wrath.

It is no revelation then that VK today wholly credits Neelam for being his strongest pillar of strength. He is acutely aware of the personal sacrifices she has made for him, and for the family. 'We've lived together for the last 25 years as brother and sister because of my physical condition, not as man and wife. That's a big sacrifice on her part as a woman,' he says candidly, giving a sense of how deeply appreciative he is of his wife's decision to stand by him through hardship.

The hunt, meanwhile for a doctor who could prescribe a therapy continued. VK was not one to easily give up and with the help of a colleague at JK, he had continued correspondence with top neurological institutes across the world. It was a reply to one of his letters from a doctor in the UK (whose name he no longer remembers), sometime in 1981, that would significantly alter the course of his life.

It would give him the profession in which lay his cure. It

would give him the profession which would shape the destiny of thousands of students, and of a declining town.

A TEACHER IS BORN

The letter began like most others did. Categorically warning him not to harbor false hopes, saying there was no cure to the disease he was suffering from. But, unlike others, it did not stop there. In it contained ten ideas for alternate professions a person with muscular dystrophy could consider, to improve quality of life. The doctor asked VK to mull over switching his job and do something that required limited mobility. Among the professions he suggested was a clerical role at a government firm, a petrol pump agency and something else that immediately triggered a chemical rush in VK's mind—coaching at home.

'COACHING AT HOME—the words solved the whole differential equation of my life!' exclaims VK.

VK felt as if a sinking ship had been rescued, as if the shore was in sight. It gave him a glimmer of hope, he felt like a man without hands, who had discovered the ability to eat with his feet. The happiness couldn't be contained and he literally became mad.

And that in a nutshell is how V.K. Bansal—a JK Synthetics engineer, became a mathematics coach.

The letter was received just as his muscle ailment was worsening and his job as assistant engineer at JK Synthetics was on the line, as a second fall due to the dystrophy threatened to render him unfit to carry on with work. VK told his wife Neelam to spread the word among her kitty party ladies that her husband was available to take mathematics tuitions in his spare time.

A single student came and VK started his home coaching service at his dining table. The boy, Puneet, who'd otherwise fail all subjects barring English, stood eighteenth in class under Bansal's tutelage. Word spread. Two more boys joined the following year. And then as news about an incredible math teacher in the JK Housing Colony travelled, dozens more thronged his house.

'*Neelam ne sirf ek chakka lagaya...aur baki ki poori match maine sambhali*,' he says smilingly in Hindi, drawing a cricketing analogy to his life's trajectory. His wife's boundary shot changed the entire course of the game.

It truly did, because, even though he hadn't begun charging his students any money yet, sons and daughters as they were of his colleagues, the goodwill he created by tutoring the kids literally saved him his job. And later, his life.

In 1983 VK was laid off. Panic ensued and he would have literally been on the streets with his family in tow had it not been for Chandrakant Agrawal, a student whose affinity towards him saved the day. Chandrakant's father, RK Agrawal was a senior manager at DCM and when his son told him about VK's plight, he agreed to use his influence and draft a mercy appeal to Sohan Lal Singhania, asking him to reconsider the decision to sack him.

Another student, Satyen Bajpai, got his father, M.C.

Bajpai—a director at another big company and someone who wielded considerable influence—to hand over the letter personally to Lalji, who sat in Kanpur.

A two year extension was granted and VK was shifted from plant to projects, a desk role that would give him ample time to prepare question papers and source mathematical problems. When the JK factory was forced to shut down for six months in 1984, VK diligently utilized the time to hone his teaching skills, even as his colleagues passed time guzzling cups of *chai* and eating Kota's famous *kachoris*. And it was providence that in 1985, the management team that had decided to give him the sack was booted out and M.C. Bajpai himself became the overall in-charge of the projects division.

'The first thing he did was tore Lalji's letter that had extended my term by only two years and assured me that my job was safe till he was around,' remembers VK.

But so popular had VK become in J.K. Colony as a teacher by 1985 that he didn't really need the job. His income from tuitions had begun matching his salary from JK. He stopped teaching school kids altogether and only began accepting students for class 11th and 12th.

'It was G.D. Agarwal of the then iconic Agarwal classes who encouraged my idea for classroom coaching,' says VK. 'His correspondence courses were very popular and he happened to be the brother-in-law of my neighbor Mr Singhal. He was visiting Kota and when I went next door to meet him, he told me to restrict my focus to competitive entrance exams and carve a niche for myself as a mathematics tutor.'

The suggestion paid rich dividends. Barely four years after he began teaching Puneet, VK sent his first student to IIT in 1986. And then several more by 1990. In 1991, the year India celebrated the dawn of liberalization, he lost his job finally. But, by then he had nearly a hundred students in seven batches and was making twice the money he did at JK.

Also teaching had begun giving him a lot more than mere pecuniary support.

LIFE IN A TRANCE

The morning of his first day after being sacked, VK sat by the window watching the hustle and bustle of known faces in the colony heading to the factory. He felt acutely depressed, not knowing what to do with his time. His batches began only in the afternoons and he had the entire morning free. For the first time after a long while, he began thinking about his disease. He had crossed 40 years of age and his condition was worsening by the day. He had started needing support to walk even short distances. The end could be lurking, he felt. The only medicine to keeping unconstructive thoughts from entering his head so far had been work, and now that very remedy had been snatched from under his feet.

Just when he felt a sob tearing from his throat he heard a knock at the door. 'Six girls appeared all of a sudden and told me their class had been shifted to the afternoons. They wondered if I could be kind enough give them extra coaching in the mornings. It was a strange twist of fate,' he says.

VK had by then begun selecting students by rejection and would only concentrate on smart kids with genuine ability. But he eased that restriction this time.

'How many girls?' he asked.

'24 of us,' said one of the girls in the group.

'Come back in the afternoon and deposit your fees in that case in the corner,' he told them, pointing to the metal box on the table to his left. By rule, he never accepted cash with his hands.

It was a massive bounty of Rs 28,800, (Rs 1200 per head)—enough money to ease the anxiety he felt in the morning. It dawned on him though that more than the riches it was the joy he felt about being given the opportunity to dedicate two more hours of the day to teaching that energized him more. His depression evaporated.

'Teaching became my savior,' he says. 'I could reclaim my life because I could teach, interact, impart knowledge, earn people's respect, laugh with the kids. The positive hormones that this generated extended my life.'

The disease, rather than hampering, had begun his capacity to live and to teach better. 'No one can teach better than me because they have other distractions. My lack of mobility forced me to concentrate all my energies on kids, so I became India's best known math tutor. As a consequence of this profession I spoke a lot, so my lungs were exercised. I also used my hands more than other people did, so my muscles remained strong. This was a medicine in disguise.'

His physical deficiency strengthened his mental faculties as well and VK narrates how the years passed by in a virtual trance as his being was engulfed by problems of algebra, geometry, and probability. He would solve problems in his dreams, and if before he woke up, he hadn't found a solution, he'd finish it before he brushed his teeth.

'*Sapne woh nahi hote jo hum sone pe dekhte hai, Sapne woh hote hai jo hume sone nahi dete hai,*' VK says.

At one point his obsession became so pathological that his wife abandoned him for a few days. But nothing would register. It was a form of creative madness and students benefitted hugely from this one track mind. When Pramod, his brother came one day to tell him it was time for them to begin looking for a match for Pooja, VK's eldest daughter, he reprimanded him.

'Get lost idiot, don't disturb me,' he said. 'Get her married to a beggar for all I care.' It wasn't that he didn't love Pooja, but so consumed was he by his love for teaching that he couldn't bear the thought of wasting time on routine homely matters. Everything from the kids' parent teacher meetings, to their illness, and their marriages were thus taken care of by Pramod and Neelam.

'When the Pandit told me the mahurat for Pooja's marriage was 4.30 am, I said I couldn't stay because I had class later that day.' The family, especially his children, whose needs he guiltily admits to have ignored, busy as he became with classes, coped with this madness and didn't hold grudges. They understood that his health and his vocation had become so intricately linked to one another that it was difficult for him to focus on anything else other than teaching.

No surprise then that on the very day he asked his class in a lecture on probability what chance there was that he would get a heart attack in the next 24 hours, he got one. It was a spooky co-incidence and even when he realized that he would collapse because of the stroke, he completed the problem on the blackboard and then got himself admitted to the hospital.

'The first question I asked the cardiologist after my heart bypass surgery was when I could begin lectures again.' He is today long past the 40 years that doctors at AIIMS had given him to live. And at 65, though bound to a wheelchair and unable any longer to walk, he remains an oft quoted example in medical circles of how a devastating disorder like muscular dystrophy can be conquered with willpower, discipline and zest for life.

INSTITUTING A LEGACY

In the decade between 1991 and 2000, VK saw success that was unparalleled, perhaps, for a teacher. He shifted out of the colony into a small house he had purchased in Kota's Vigyan Nagar area a few years prior, fearing the possibility that landlords wouldn't be too encouraged to rent out a place to a handicapped, retired person. It is here that Bansal Classes Pvt. Ltd was officially institutionalized with external teachers brought in to also teach physics and chemistry along with mathematics, which was VK's domain.

'Had it not been for another institute Career Point, I wouldn't conceivably have formally started a coaching institute,' admits VK.

It is an interesting story—one that has two versions. That of V.K. Bansal, and Pramod Maheshwari, the IITan entrepreneur who founded the publicly listed coaching academy Career Point in 1993. It was the turf war between these two educators-turned-businessmen that truth be told, laid the foundations for formalizing the coaching set up in Kota, which till 1995 was still a small home scale effort. Had the two not bickered, perhaps coaching wouldn't have reached the scale it has today.

'I knew Maheshwari was an excellent Physics teacher and so would refer my students to him. There was an unwritten understanding between us that he would teach physics and I would teach math. But out of the blue one day, he told his students that if they wanted to learn physics from him, they would also mandatorily have to study math and chemistry at his institute. I only retaliated and put the same conditions on my students,' says VK.

Maheshwari on his part accuses VK of first laying down such diktats, insecure as he was by the headway Career Point was making.

Whatever may be the truth, thus began the era of coaching institutes in Kota. And what ensued was a hyper competitive game of one-upmanship in which VK emerged the clear victor, relegating Career Point to the number two position for the longest time. It is impossible to verify numbers, given how spuriously they are brandied about in Kota, but every credible source in the town vouches for the dominion VK held all the way from the latter half of the 90s up to 2008, when coaching was in a sense synonymous with Bansal Classes.

The rivalry only helped Kota. As Maheshwari and VK put in all their effort into churning out more and more IITans, the town began coming into prominence as a coaching hub to reckon with. In 1997 Bansal and Career Point collectively sent 200 students to IIT sparking enormous interest in the local media. From Ajmer to Udaipur, Sawai Madhopur to Alwar, students flocked the town as news of Kota's successful coaching techniques made headlines.

To accommodate the growing numbers VK began buying one piece of land after another, till he owned six properties in which the coaching academy was housed. As the number of students increased by the year, new floors were added. By the turn of the new century the dining table had morphed into classrooms where VK and other top notch faculty members became guiding lights for nearly 5,000 students of physics, chemistry, and math, who had come there with a hope of cracking that thorny IIT entrance test.

The town of Kota found a fresh spring to latch on to. J.K's closure in 1997 had crippled its economy, and coaching brought with it a new dawn for this ancient Rajput kingdom. The hubbub in the 1990s was just a precursor though. The real explosion of coaching institutes happened by the turn of the new century when in 2000, two of VK's students Nitin Gupta and Varun Kacholia obtained the All India Ranks (AIR)

1 and 2 in the IIT JEE test and the total number of selections hit the 300 mark.

That, well and truly changed Kota's fortunes and those of VK.

THE MILLENNIAL EXPLOSION

Bansal Classes became a nationally recognized name overnight.

A week after Nitin Gupta's results were announced in the May of 2000, VKs younger brother, Pramod, who had by 1997 joined his brother's flourishing business after losing his job at JK, remembers having to call the police. Large crowds had gathered outside the coaching centre in 2K-70 Vigyan Nagar, hoping to admit their kids into the academy and there was chaos as the guards were unable to control the mob.

'I was busy in the office preparing the selection tests for the 12th standard students when I heard a commotion outside the building. News of a small coaching institute in Kota having aided a small town boy from Bharatpur to achieve rank one in the all India JEE test had spread like wild fire. It had made national headlines prompting people from as far off as Bihar and UP to come to Kota and witness firsthand what was going on.'

They numbered in thousands, and when Pramod finally came out to announce that admission slots for that year were already filled, crowds got violent. So desperate were some people that they wrote demand drafts with their phone numbers at the back side and threw them past the gate. Others offered on spot donations. VK refused. Entry would be granted only to those that passed the Bansal Classes entrance test.

Those were the glory days when the acceptance ratio at Bansal Classes was 1:10, when a student would be admitted keeping in mind his aptitude and not the institute's capacity and infrastructure or turnover targets.

For the very first time that day though VK got a sense of the power of the All India Rank, and from then on there was no looking back. Concentrating his energies on training only the brightest of students with real aptitude, he took Bansal Classes from strength to strength producing top rankers (AIR 1 to 3) year after year consecutively till 2009. From a single student on the dining table in 1981, VK had a strength of twenty five thousand students under his guidance by 2008. He reached a crescendo of success that year with the institute clocking a turnover of Rs 1.2 billion and establishing an unbeatable record of having secured the futures of thousands of IIT aspirants.

He also became a cult figure of sorts.

THE V.K. METHOD

VK's recurring success in sending large number of students every year to the IITs roused suspicion among officials there. There were genuine doubts even that papers were being leaked to him. It was only after some time passed that people's misgivings were laid to rest and they began to recognize that it wasn't deceit, but tremendous hard work and application of mind put into codifying the precise requirements needed to crack the exam convention that was responsible for his consistent track record.

He had a razor-sharp understanding of the boundary of probability of a particular kind of question appearing and taught his students accordingly. 'He administers a right dose and the material that's been developed here over the years is one of a kind,' says a student from Mumbai.

VK would scan hundreds of books at trade fairs, order material from overseas and refer to material accessed from obscure texts before he formulated his problem sheets. He also instituted the DPP (daily practice problems) sheets, a revision mechanism through which students were expected to answer 10 surprise problems based on previous chapters as they waited for their next lecture.

This is a system that's now been widely replicated by all other coaching centers in Kota. And VK even accuses other institutes of blatantly copying his unique methodology and says the so-called Kota technique pioneered by him has now percolated its way through the entire coaching industry.

While he was developing teaching technique, the one silent force working behind-the-scenes during these years was his younger brother Pramod. He was the executor, the backend force that ensured that his brother faced no hitch. Between the two, they created perfect symphony—VK as the teacher and PK as Pramod came to be known, as the administrator—helping Bansal Classes cross one milestone after another.

As a child, when Pramod had found out about VK's incapacitating condition, he had made a resolve to move to Kota so he could be of help to his brother. Luckily he was absorbed into JK as an engineer and so lived with the family contributing very early on to their needs. He'd drive VK to and from the factory, on an old Lambretta scooter, attend the parent-teacher meetings of his nieces and nephew, help VK with his tuitions after coming home at 5 pm and do every other odd job that was asked of him. He really did everything apart from the actual teaching—from cyclostyling and photocopying question papers, scheduling batches to collecting fees.

The same role was magnified multifold when Bansal Classes was institutionalized and Pramod assumed the role of CEO. And he brought along with him a vision to take the establishment to new heights commercially. By 2007, Pramod moved operations to a swanky 3,50,000 sq ft coaching centre named Gaurav Towers that could accommodate thirty thousand students. It became an insignia of the success his brother had achieved with its 120 air-conditioned classrooms, cafeterias, recreation facilities and state of the art technology available for learning.

He was weary of expanding too quickly because the nucleus of the business was VK and Pramod was acutely aware that his physical condition could give way anytime. It was only when a senior faculty member from Delhi, who had come visiting to the Vigyan Nagar institute related his disappointment at the rather modest dimensions of a nationally renowned coaching academy like Bansal, that a decision was taken to move to a building that had the scale and character fit for a premier coaching hub of the country.

Special permissions were granted to VK by the Chief Minister to also build his residence in the same compound despite the location of the academy being in the Indraprastha Industrial Area.

SPWANING A WEB OF ENTERPRISE

Indraprastha Industrial Area is also home to the gleaming towers of other coaching institutes. And VK's most significant contribution to the field of education has not been that he has sent thousands (18,000 odd at last count) of young dreamers to India's premier technology institute, but that he spawned a wide web of enterprise in Kota. His success sowed the seeds for many others to follow suit. Hundreds of other coaching centers came up and added to these thousands, creating a multiplier effect.

Classroom coaching was virtually non-existent at the time he began, but several centers sprouted in Kota capitalizing on his fame—Allen Career Institute in the late 80s, Career Point in the mid 90s, Resonance in early 2000s, Vibrant in 2007 and at least a couple of hundred other less prominent offshoots—comprising often of faculty from Bansal's own backyard branching out, but sometimes original entrepreneurs inspired by his success as well. All of them contributed to formalizing coaching and gave Kota the distinction of being called India's education city which according to a Times of India report sent a lion's share of 7000 selections against a total of 27,151 selections for the 9500 seats across IITs in 2014.

Every activity in Kota today, is centered around its students. They are Kota's mainstay and have been for the last decade and half when it began rising to prominence. Coaching has enabled a whole set of ancillary industries to press forward here as well and from the schedules of auto rickshaws that ply between the shiny towers of the institutes and the plentiful student PGs and hostels in Rajiv Gandhi Nagar, to the myriad messes that feed them, to photocopy and stationary stalls at the end of every street to City Mall on Road No. 1 that houses the best known global brands, the humble student is what makes Kota tick.

Nothing any longer is more lucrative than servicing the needs of the coaching industry which has in the two decades since it was institutionalized garnered such an alarming scale that an entire town thrives on its takings.

'The *jalebi* and *poha thelawala* in Vigyaan Nagar opens at 4 am so that the 5 am batch can eat before class,' says Sumeet Chaturvedi, who opened a hotel cum serviced apartment—Leisure Inn—last year to cater to growing demand for better quality accommodation in town. His story encapsulates the success of many others who've benefited from the coaching institutes. Chaturvedi's mother began providing lunch to students in the late 1990s, then started a mess called *Khana*

Khazana. As her sons grew up they got into the hostels management business as an extension of the services their mother offered and have now finally got down to owning their own hotel as demands from parents for superior lodging infrastructure grew.

'Every other enterprise has fallen by the periphery. Students come first,' says a housewife-turned-beautician, who has watched her business scale new heights every passing year. Just on the day of my arrival, there is news that an agarbatti manufacturer has shuttered his factory to convert it into a student hostel. And the oft repeated joke here is that residents in this town's prime areas even vacate their homes and live in rental apartments so as to accommodate students. Such is the power of their penny.

'TO LET' signs are visible outside every home and many seem to have undergone some kind of makeshift late addition—a new floor, an extended bedroom, a toilet—to lodge the nearly 100,000 students that still make their way to Kota every year.

VK can claim a lot of credit for this and it is an achievement he is proud of, an achievement that by the way, Kota itself never lets him forget. Nearly every screaming billboard in town, plastered with mugs of the most sought after faculty or 'sirs' has a proud 'ex-Bansal' label to it—testimony of the lasting imprint he will leave behind, and the strong brand he has built, no matter that the last few years have been a rough ride for his institute.

THE TROUGH

Every success story has its dark side. And with opportunity for prosperity opened several avenues for corruption in Kota, which somewhere along the way fell prey, becoming an *adda* of sorts for the worst kind of depravity. Competition also intensified exponentially and in the madding crowd, Bansal Classes lost out, becoming a diminished version of the roaring success it once was, constrained as VK was by his principles from engaging in the brazenly unscrupulous practices some of his competitors began indulging in.

Between 2009 and 2014, even while it continued to maintain its record of producing roughly 10 percent of IIT entrants, Bansal Classes couldn't manage the high ranks it once produced. Student volumes plummeted as a result from 25,000 in 2008 to roughly 7000-8000 per annum and other newer establishments strode ahead of Bansal, casting a shadow over its luminous past.

What went wrong? Plenty. A distorted market proliferated with debauched entities, mass exodus of faculty members as well as shortsightedness on part of VKto sniff a change in the market among other things. Changing patterns of the IIT - JEE exams also proved costly.

In 2000, three of Bansal's key teaching staff—R.K. Verma, B.V. Rao, and Shishir Mittal—branched out and formed Resonance. The following year eight other senior teachers quit, precipitating a crisis of sorts. Aside of VK and Pooja, his eldest daughter, who had by then joined Bansal Classes, only Nitin Jain—a faculty for physics remained. It became a matter of great urgency to find quick replacements and VK told his students to give him three days. A loss of face was averted at the last minute when a renowned teacher from Jaipur—Ashish Arora—knocked on VK's door, asking whether he could be given a job.

But Bansal wasn't as lucky in the following years. In 2009, nine teachers quit in concert and founded Vibrant Academy. In the interim, several other institutes also poached faculty from the Bansal pool, luring them with fat pay packets that went up to as high as Rs 2 cr per annum. The biggest blow came in 2011, when Allan Career Institute, which is today at the top as a result of its niche in the pre-medical segment, poached a solid 30 teachers from VK's stable, literally crippling his operations. Students migrated along with teachers and the perception that Bansal no longer had good teachers held solid.

VK admits quite candidly that his ego came in the way of stopping good faculty from leaving. And neither was much done to improve bench strength in order to deal with another exodus. '*Ravan ko abhimaan aagaya tha ki muje koi nahi hara sakta*,' he admits.

If this phenomenon was bad enough, what was worse was the practice that took steam of luring students that were potential rankers with large sums of money. Early this year news about an IIT JEE top ranker being felicitated with a cheque for Rs 21 lakh made the top story in local papers. He was poached a year earlier from Bansal Classes by a rival institute, so that his success could be capitalized on and advertised in publicity hoardings to attract more students. The commoditization of education had reached its pinnacle.

'Things have taken a 180 degree turnaround,' says PK. 'I remember a time when students would be distributing *mithai* post results, now institutes have begun handing out sweets (or cheques).'

But hyper competition had begun pushing the coaching industry to employ all sorts of dirty tactics long before this incident. The student was commoditized the day that fine distinction between teaching and business blurred. And here's where VK failed as an entrepreneur, his educator mindset unable to reconcile to the reality that he needed to do other things aside of teaching brilliantly—heavy duty marketing, effective brand building and rapid expansion—in order to remain at the forefront.

Bansal Classes faltered on all these counts. It didn't for instance advertise enough, or put out as many hoardings as its rivals showcasing their success stories, or plan a strategy to counter the vicious marketing gimmicks they used against it to get ahead.

'I am a teacher first, and then a businessman. And I do believe that in the long run that is what will matter,' he still asserts in what is perhaps a warning for Kota's coaching factories about the approach they will need to espouse if they are to remain relevant in the long run. Only recently has he given in to the pulls and pressures of the market, and allowed his marketing team to spruce up their activities.

But a competitor who is today in a far better position than VK, also attributes his concentration solely on the brightest of pupils in the initial years for the current decline his institute is witnessing.

'Beyond the fact that they didn't concentrate on brand building, VK focused only on the top 10 percent. The remaining 90 percent always felt alienated and would be happily absorbed by other institutes. That was okay till 2009 when Bansal Classes was consistently producing top rankers. But the virtuous cycle was broken the day a faculty exodus happened and certain good students chose to go along to another institute with their teachers.'

The year 2009 was also when VK got his stroke, and his capacities deteriorated considerably. VK's cult status, his overpowering personality had relegated other faculty to the shadows. And this dependence of the institute on his celebrity status switched from being an asset to a liability as he took a backseat.

'Bansal Classes without V.K. Bansal was like a film without a hero. The protagonist himself was no longer at the vanguard, making only guest appearances, and others weren't significant enough to drive our USP,' analyzes one executive.

It took longer than it should have for both PK and VK to realize that all of these issues were harming them to a great extent. Luckily two years ago they begun making amends, and are slowly riding out of the slump.

RECLAIMING GLORY

Sameer Bansal is a carbon copy of his dad, a younger VK. He is director at Bansal Classes and a popular mathematics tutor at the institute. VK. teaches only one batch a day these days, his health not permitting him to exert very much. Upon Sameer's shoulders now rests the responsibility of recouping his father's towering legacy. It is a daunting task and Sameer is wholly conscious of what it means to inherit this job.

'I'd draw the Abhishek Bachchan—Amitabh Bachchan parallel here,' he articulates, insisting that he can never be as effective as his father. Not only did VK exert a great degree of power and influence upon students and teachers, but times in general were different. The teacher-taught relationship today is no longer what it used to be. It is more a contractor-client transaction resulting in a radical culture shift at the coaching institutes. It is their own doing, their rabid commercialization bid eroding the sanctity of learning. And Sameer is now finding it tough to revive the culture that his father once instituted in Kota.

At any rate, Bansal Classes continues to remain among the top five in spite of the challenges of the oligopolistic market, no matter that it is struggling to recapture the top spot. But VK considers Sameer a worthy successor, a real replacement for him, someone who he believes will show results in time.

His two daughters Pooja and Arti have also done him proud. They handle the Jaipur and Ajmer divisions of Bansal Classes today. Daughter-in law Mahima is a director and faculty member as well, so in some sense his teaching genes have spread far and wide within the family fold, all of whom collectively hold the responsibility as the guardians of the flame.

There is much that the Bansals have collectively done in the last two years to give a new lease of life to their father's institute. For one the poaching phenomenon is being addressed on a war footing. Twelve senior teachers have been made partners, retained on a profit sharing basis as directors, rather than as salaried employees, so as to make them stakeholders in the institute's success or failure. This has brought about a great deal of stability to operations. Instances of poaching have reduced and not a single teacher has left Bansal Classes in the past two years.

'If we maintain this record for another two-three years, I have no doubt in my mind that we will reclaim our top position once more. The perception that teachers leave us needs to be conquered. Once we do that it will be difficult to beat us,' insists Sameer.

For an establishment that once shunned billboards, hoardings and advertised only twice a year—during the results and at the time of admissions, brand building and promotions now play important roles in making people aware of their achievements. Yet, it is a far cry from what rivals do—hyper promotional activities, negative publicity of competitors etc.

'Bansal sir still hates the word marketing and when we go and talk to him about the potential of a certain "catchment area" he flares up,' laughs a faculty member. But tough times call for tough measures and he has eased up a little to the concept, even though he continues to believe that branding can only be supplementary to what used to be the real USP of Kota—good quality education.

With a growing trend of decentralization, proactive steps have also been taken to expand footprint outside Kota and make requisite investments in virtual and distance education. Through their own establishments and through franchisees, Bansal Classes now has facilities in 20 cities from Meerut to Mathura and Bhilai to Bareilly. Five more cities will be added every year.

'One way to analyze this would be that the significance of Kota—once considered the Mecca of learning is diminishing. The other way would be to look at it as the Kota philosophy propounded by Bansal sir is being lifted out of its geographical constraints, to be spread out far and wide,' says an observer. But here too, competitors like Resonance have made a much faster headway and VK will have to do a lot of catching up.

While every effort is clearly being made to respond to the changing market, VK says he isn't overly bothered about the rat race. He would never surrender his core principles to ensure that his institute remains in business anyway. 'I'd rather shut shop and go out of circulation than remain relevant at any cost,' says VK. 'My students are my biggest advertisement and if they stop saying good things about us, which I hope they won't, then I have no right to survive.'

'Highs and lows are part of life,' he adds, getting philosophical. 'Strength of students shouldn't ultimately decide who is number one. Our prime endeavor will be to produce top results once again and not by padding up our numbers or poaching faculty and luring class 11 rankers from other institutes with money to come and join us so that we can capitalize on their name. Not because I can't. It is easy for me to spend a few crores and do all of this, but what for? I don't want a house on the moon.'

The satisfaction he derives from the reverse energy that flows sometimes when a student solves a problem he's taught using a shorter method far exceeds a burgeoning bank balance clearly. And more than anything else VK cherishes the act of teaching, of interacting with students in his spare time, of having an odd lunch with them, of caring for those that reside in the hostel Bansal Classes has recently built when they are unwell.

'I call the girls over sometimes for an ice cream, or send homemade khichadi to their room if they aren't keeping well,' he says. 'For a wheelchair bound individual who cannot spend money on travel or extravagant hobbies, these are my simple pleasures.'

Not too many others of his stature would invest so much time in building personal relationships with students, who are in Kota often looked at today as raw material to be exploited for profit. But VK's monetary ambitions have always been modest. At a time when his rivals of a far lesser distinction were lapping up hundreds of crores in private equity money, he steered clear from it because this is a business in which one earns first and then spends.

'I wonder why they needed to raise money,' he says, insisting that he hasn't ever taken a loan in his life. Even the massive five acre campus of Gaurav Towers was built with the cash that the company already held in its kitty.

There is a special reason for this aversion to assuming debt. As a patient for muscular dystrophy, VK always felt comfortable psychologically with having liquid cash. 'What if a cure is found and I don't have money for the surgery?' he asks with a childlike sincerity, and then gazes outside his window with a twitch in his eyebrow, as the hullaballoo of students laughing and talking as they step into the building for his class distracts him.

He looks forward to a day when these corridors of knowledge will produce that elusive AIR 1 once more, he says, pushing his automatic wheel chair towards the door.

'In that and nowhere else lies the true gauge of an institute's success.'

ACKNOWLEDGMENTS

I wish, first and foremost, to express gratitude to the men featured in this book for allowing me access to their lives. I am infinitely grateful also to their friends, family, and colleagues for sparing invaluable time talking to me. Their communications teams deserve a special mention for being ever so helpful in coordinating dates and logistics—Mahasweta Sen, Lalima Bose, and Modali Venkat Hari Kishen in particular.

I thank Arun Maheshwari for letting me draw on his book for further insights into the life of R.S. Agarwal, Jency Jacob for suggesting that I take up this challenge, my bosses at Business Standard for being so flexible about my schedules, and Debdatta Das for giving me her ear always.

Last but certainly not the least this endeavor would've been impossible without encouragement and support from my parents and family.